SOUND MIND;

OR,

CONTRIBUTIONS

TO THE

NATURAL HISTORY AND PHYSIOLOGY

OF THE

HUMAN INTELLECT.

By JOHN HASLAM, M.D.

PREFACE.

The indulgence of the public has been already extended to several works which I have submitted to its decision on the subject of Insanity; and the same favourable interpretation is now solicited for the present performance,—which attempts the more difficult investigation of Sound Mind. In treating of Mental Derangement, I became very early sensible, that a competent knowledge of the faculties and operations of the Intellect in its healthy state, was indispensably necessary to him, who professed to describe its disorders:—that in order to define the aberrations, the standard should be fixed. There was indeed no lack of theories and systems of Metaphysic; and although they essentially differed, many possessed the highest reputation. Amidst this distraction of conflicting opinions, which no mediator could adequately reconcile,— without daring to contend with a host of discrepancies, or presuming to demolish the lofty edifices which scholastic Pneumatology had reared,—I determined to throw off the shackles of authority, and think for myself. For it was evident, on the freehold ground of literature, that there is "ample room and verge enough" for every man to build his own tenement;—and the present construction is too lowly to intercept another's prospect, and without those ornaments that might provoke the jealousy, or challenge the rivalship of surrounding inhabitants.

The mind of every rational person may be considered as an elaboratory, wherein he may conduct psychological experiments:—he is enabled to analyze his own acquirement,—and if he be sufficiently attentive, he may note its formation and progress in his children:—and thus trace the accumulation of knowledge, from the dawn of infancy to the meridian of manhood. The prosecution of these means, according to my own views, will qualify the diligent observer, to become the Natural Historian and Physiologist of the Human Mind.

In the comparative survey of the capacities of Man, and the intelligence of animals, the contrast has appeared so striking, that it was impossible wholly to abstain from the inference of his future destination:—notwithstanding very different conclusions had been extorted by some modern physiologists. It has been often remarked, that the practitioners of the healing art, have been very moderately impressed with a solicitude for the future. This observation, in some late instances, has been unhappily confirmed:—but it would be unjust to visit the whole tribe with a sweeping and acrimonious censure, for the transgressions of a few. The reproach has, however, long existed. The venerable father of English poetry, in his description of the Doctor, has passed a high and merited compliment to his learning; which at that period was a heterogeneous compound of Greek, Latin, and Arabian lore, mysteriously engrafted on Galenicals and Astrology:—yet with this courteous concession to his professional science he could not refrain from a dry and sarcastic memorandum, that

"His study was but little in the Bible."

Throughout this inquiry, the province of the Theologian has never been invaded:—it has been my humble toil to collect and concentrate the scattered rays which emanate from natural reason,—a pale phosphoric light, and "uneffectual" glow, compared with the splendid and animating beams, which issue from the source of divine communication.

As the object of these contributions, has been principally to convey my opinions, concerning the formation of the human mind, from the superior capacities that man possesses, many subjects have been left untouched, which, in similar works, urge an important claim to the attention of the reader. Among these neglected articles, theImagination is the chief omission:—of which many authors have treated so copiously, and so well. According to my own views, the consideration of this faculty was not essential to the outline that has been traced;—and it has been rather deemed a graceful embellishment, than a constituent pillar of the edifice of mind. This gay attirer of thought, that decks passion and sentiment, is also the prolific parent of fiction;—and justly banished from the retreats of sober demonstration.—To the science of numbers,—to mathematical precision, and to the whole range of experimental philosophy,—Imagination does not lend her glowing and gaudy tints. No vestiges of her colouring can be discovered in Divine ordinances, or in the systems of human jurisprudence:—neither in the Ten Commandments nor in the Statutes at Large. Imagination may indeed enliven the cold pages of historical narrative, and blend the "Utile Dulci"—but even here she is a profane intruder: and a vigilant eye must be directed, lest, in some unguarded moment, her seductive blandishments should decoy the nakedness of truth. A sedate and unambitious recorder of facts, does not presume to describe her regions, or to enumerate her attributes. That delightful task must be performed by her votaries,

"The poet, the lunatic, and the lover;"

nor should the Orator be excluded from his fair participation and kindred alliance with this airy and fascinating group.

If the present essay should conform to nature, and be founded in truth,—should it assist the young inquirer, and more especially the medical student,—for whom no compendium of the science of mind has been hitherto prepared; my own expectations will be fully answered; and this scantling may probably lead some more capable person to an extensive investigation, enlarged comprehension, and luminous arrangement of the phenomena of the human intellect.

JOHN HASLAM.

57. Frith-Street, Soho-Square,
    1st November, 1819.

CONTENTS.

SOUND MIND.

PERCEPTION.

The faculty of perceiving the objects which surround us, is an important feature in the history of mind; but by what means or contrivance this is effected, can only be known to the Supreme Being, who has thus been pleased to endow us; and our utmost endeavours to detect the *modus operandi* will be puerile and unavailing.

The first operations of the infant are to educate its senses, in order to become acquainted, through these organs, with surrounding objects. This, in the human species, is a process of very slow attain ment; and our information concerning this subject, must be derived from attentively watching the progress of the infant itself; as of these early perceptions, for a reason which will be afterwards assigned, we retain no distinct recollection.

For the manner in which we become acquainted with the objects in nature, we have appropriated a term, which was probably supposed to be explanatory of the process, by which we received our intelligence of these phenomena, and have accordingly termed it *Perception*. The intrinsic meaning of this word is the taking, seizing, or grasping, of an object, from the Latin *Cum* and *Capio*, and the same figure pervades most of the European languages. This term may sufficiently apply to the information we derive from the organ of touch; but it affords no solution of that which we obtain through the medium of the other senses, as sight, smell, and hearing. It has been the bane of philosophy, and the great obstacle to its advancement, that we have endeavoured to penetrate that

1

which is inscrutable; and in this vain pursuit, we have neglected to detect and cultivate that which is obvious, and the legitimate province of our research.

These organs of sense are the instruments by which we obtain our different perceptions; they are the tests by which we become acquainted with the objects of nature.

When we view the newly-born infant, and consider its state for many weeks after it has become a member of our community, we are then enabled to form some opinion of the almost insensible gradations, by which it acquires its perceptions. An enumeration of the progressive steps of this tardy process is within the power of any patient and accurate observer; but this detail does not constitute a part of the plan which has been adopted.

It has been endeavoured by writers on this subject, to establish a distinction between perception and sensation, and the reader for his information may consult their works: they do not however appear to have founded this distinction on any obvious difference, nor to have adduced sufficient reasons for their separate establishment, as independent properties of the nerves. To feel, to experience a sensation, or to perceive, implies consciousness; it is that which is transmitted by the nerves to the sensorium, either by the organs of sense, or by the internal nerves; as pain, or feelings of which we are conscious. Consciousness is the test, the evidence, the proof of sensation or perception. This point has been adverted to, in order that terms should not be multiplied without a distinct and essential difference of meaning.

The five senses, together with some auxiliaries, which will be the subjects of future notice, may be considered as the instruments or agents, by which the edifice of mind is constructed. In the act of perceiving by the different senses, there are some circumstances, which are particularly deserving of attention. In order that perception may fully and certainly take place, it is necessary that the person should be undisturbed; he ought to be exempt from external intrusions, and internal perturbation. During this process the respiration is in general more slowly drawn, the body endeavours to maintain a perfect quietude, and its position becomes fixed. When we perceive objects by the eye, this organ becomes fixed and the lips are usually closed. During our examinations by the touch, the eye is also fixed, the breathing is suspended, and the lips brought into contact: the fingers are separated, and their more delicately tangent surfaces applied to the object with their utmost expansion. In the exercise of audible perception, the neck is stretched forth, and the ear applied to the quarter from whence the sound appears to issue; the mouth is partly open to conduct the vibrations to the Eustachian tube. When we acquire intelligence by the smell, the lips are very firmly closed, the nostrils become dilated, and the inspiration of air through them is conducted by short and successive inhalations. From the connection between the smell and organs of taste, (and this association is more remarkable in some animals than in man,) it is difficult to describe the process, which, however, principally consists, when minutely tasting, in moving the tongue (the principal discriminator) on the palate:—but when urged by strong appetite as in the act of feeding, and when divested of the restraints which refined society imposes; the nostrils are widely expanded, the eye is keenly directed to the portion, and the hands are busily employed.

Experience has sufficiently informed us that the organs of sense must be in a healthy state, in order to the due conveyance of perception. When the function of any organ is altogether defective, as when a person is born blind, he is cut off from all perception of light and of visible objects. If by nature deaf, from the intonation of sounds; and many unhappy instances of such connate defects abound among our species. In one particular subject, both these defects existed from birth; so that the sum of his intelligence was conveyed by the touch, smell, and taste, or in other words, his mind was exclusively composed of the perceptions he derived from these senses. This case will be more particularly noticed in a subsequent chapter. The alterations which take place in the state of our perceptions from a morbid cause, are generally known. Thus a person labouring under a catarrh, will be unable to detect the odours which certain substances communicate in a healthy condition of his olfactory organ. In fever excited by a disordered stomach, the taste will become vitiated, and the partial obstruction of the ear by accumulated wax, will impress him with the bubbling of a pot, the singing of birds, or the ringing of bells.

The same law that produces fatigue in a muscle from exertion, appears to obtain in the organs of sense. If they be excited by their appropriate stimuli too violently, or for a too long continuance, fatigue or languor is produced, their percipience is diminished, or confusedly conveyed; and they require a period of rest for their refreshment.

As we advance in our enquiries into the nature of perception, it will be evident that we cannot long continue to treat of it as a simple act, or as a distinct faculty. The organs by which we obtain our different perceptions are not insulated parts, but communicate with a substance, termed the brain, and which is continued through the vertebral column. The ultimate expansion of a nerve of sense, has been termed its sentient or percipient extremity; and where it is united to the brain, its sensorial insertion. If we were to divide the optic nerve where it passes into the foramen, taking care to leave the apparatus of the eye uninjured, the visual organ would be deprived of its function, and the person or animal would be completely blind of that eye; so that a communication with the brain is necessary for the purpose or act of perception. As therefore the union of the nerve with the brain is indispensably necessary for the purpose or act of perception, we are naturally led to inquire into the properties of this substance, termed the brain. Before we proceed to this part of the subject, it will be proper to notice a fact which is of frequent occurrence. In amputations of the thigh, at the moment the femoral nerve is divided, it often occurs that a pain is distinctly felt in the toes; and after the limb has been removed, even for many months, the same painful feeling of these lost extremities is occasionally experienced. This circumstance would render it probable that the larger branch of the nerve becomes itself impregnated with the sensation it transmits: indeed it is a continuation of the same substance, from its sentient extremity to its sensorial insertion. This intimate union of nerve and brain may be further illustrated: it has been already noticed, that a morbid state of the organs of sense will convey inaccurate perceptions; and it is equally certain, that disease of the brain, will excite phantasms, which appear as realities to the sensitive organs.

As consciousness is implied, in order to constitute the act of perception, it is of some importance to investigate the nature and meaning of this term. The consciousness of *having experienced* a perception by any of the senses would be an act of memory: consciousness, therefore, applies to the past; and it also accompanies our prediction of the future. When a person is writing a letter, he is at the time, conscious that his own hand is forming the characters; if this letter be afterwards submitted to his inspection, he is conscious that he wrote it; and if he be desired to write it over again, he is conscious that it will bear, both to himself and others, the character of his hand-writing. Consciousness, therefore, accompanies human action through all its tenses: it is equivalent to the knowledge we possess of our own personal identity, the evidence of mind, and therefore must accompany every act of intelligence. Thus we are equally conscious that we perceive, remember, think or reflect, and reason. As consciousness must accompany every act of perception, it follows that we cannot be impressed with more than one at the same instant; for it can never be contended that we are able to experience two acts of consciousness at the same moment. The very term two, implies repetition or succession, and we could as well conceive the possibility of being, at the same time, in two different places.

As far as we are warranted to infer from the evidences it affords, an infant appears to possess no consciousness; but it may be considered of early acquirement, and coeval with distinctness of perception.

These few preliminary remarks concerning perception have been submitted to the notice of the reader, in order to advance to another subject. The faculties which constitute mind are so blended, and dependant on each other, that it would only hazard confusion to proceed. But this subject will be resumed.[1]

[1] There exists already furnished, a considerable mass of facts, dispersed in various works, which might be advantageously collected into a volume in order to illustrate the phenomena and laws of perception, and more especially to display the mutual assistance they afford to each other, and the superior knowledge which we have derived from their united co-operation.

MEMORY.

Allow a human being to be gifted with his five senses, exquisitely attuned for the conveyance of those perceptions, which the separate organs and common sensory are destined to receive: let him during fifty, or as many thousand years, scent the most delicious perfumes,—convey to his palate the flavour of the choicest viands,—to his eyes, present the fairest prospects in nature,—impart to his ear the sweetest music, and regale his touch with smoothness and warmth; moreover let him be conscious of each individual perception he receives:—what would he be at the expiration of this period, without recollection? He would be no more than a sheet of white paper, that had been carried round the world to receive, through the camera obscura, its most delightful views; or the bare walls of Westminster Abbey, after the commemoration of Handel. Perception and consciousness, therefore, although indispensable to the building up of mind, are by themselves inefficient and useless without the adjunct of memory.

The writers who have treated of the human faculties, have usually and properly bestowed an elaborate investigation to the developement of this interesting subject: indeed, when men first began to describe the operations of their own minds, it might be expected that they would treat copiously of its most important function; but the nature of this endowment has received no elucidation from the aggregate of their labours.

The term memory has been Anglicised from the Latin Memoria; yet we possess two other words of similar meaning, and from their derivation, in a certain degree, explanatory of this process; namely, to REMEMBER and RECOLLECT. Thus if an individual have seen any particular animal, and given sufficient attention to perceive accurately its construction, so as to possess a complete perception of the different parts or *members* of which it is composed; he would, in the absence of the animal, be enabled to remember it. If his hand had been duly educated he might form its model, or chisel it from a block of marble; or on a plain surface, according to the rules of art, might make a drawing of the animal, and with such exactitude of its different *members*, that it would appear to those who compared it with the original, that he perfectly *re-membered* it. To recollect is only a different figure for the same process, and implies to re-gather or collect, those parts which have been scattered in different directions.

The perceptions we obtain by our different senses are all capable of being remembered, but in different ways. Those which we derive from sight, may be communicated by the pictures of the objects, which become the means of assisting our recollection, and thus form a durable record of our visible perceptions; of course excepting motion, which pictures cannot represent; but motion, or change of place, implies a succession of perceptions. Yet this manner of record does not directly apply to the other senses: we can exhibit no pictures of odours, tastes, the lowing of a cow, the roaring of a lion, or the warbling of birds; much less do hardness and softness admit of any picturesque representations as their record. The memory of animals seems to be in the simple state: they have, through their organs, different perceptions; and in many instances these organs are more susceptible than those of the human subject. The ear of some timid species is enabled to collect the feeblest vibrations of sound, and which are inaudible to us. The eye of some birds can tolerate an effulgence of light, that would dazzle and confuse our vision; and others "do their errands," in a gloom where we could not distinguish. In certain animals the smell is so acute, that it becomes a sense of the highest importance for the purposes of their destination. But animals are incapable of recording their perceptions by any signs or tokens: they therefore possess no means of recalling them, and their recollection can only be awaked from the recurrence of the object, by which the perception was originally excited: whereas man, by the possession of speech, and of the characters in which it is recorded, can at all times revive his recollection of the past.

It is generally acknowledged that our memory is in proportion to the distinctness of the perception, and also to the frequency of its repetition.

The simple acts of perception and memory appear to be the same in man and animals; and there are many facts which would induce us to suppose, if these faculties be identical in their nature, that the endowment of the latter is more excellent. This conjecture is hazarded from the greater susceptibility of the organs of some animals, and from their wonderful recollection of tracks which they have traversed. Among the phenomena of memory there are two very curious occurrences, and for which no adequate explanation has been hitherto afforded. Many of the transactions of our early years appear to be wholly obliterated from our recollection; they have never been presented as the subject of our thoughts, but after the lapse of many years, have been accidentally revived, by our being placed in the situation which originally gave them birth. Although there are numerous instances on record, and some perhaps familiar to every reader, I shall prefer the relation of one which came under my immediate observation. About sixteen years ago, I attended a lady at some distance from town, who was in the last stage of an incurable disorder. A short time before her death, she requested that her youngest child, a girl about four years of age, might be brought to visit her, and which was accordingly complied with. The child remained with her about three days. During the last summer some circumstances led me to accompany this young lady to the same house. Of her visit when a child she retained no trace of recollection, nor was the name of the village even known to her. When arrived at the house, she had no memory of its exterior; but on entering the room where her mother had been confined, her eye anxiously traversed the apartment, and she said, "I have been here before, the prospect from the window is quite familiar to me, and I remember that in this part of the room there was a bed and a sick lady, who kissed me and wept." On minute inquiry none of these circumstances had ever occurred to her recollection during this long interval, and in all probability they would never have recurred but for the locality which revived them. In a work professedly the fabric of fancy, but which is evidently a portrait from nature, and most highly finished,—in the third volume of Guy Mannering, the reader may peruse a similar but more interesting relation, where the return of Bertram to the scenes of his childhood, awakens a train of reminiscences which conduce to the developement of his history and legitimate claims. According to my own interpretation, however wonderful these phenomena of memory may appear, they merely afford examples of the simplest acts of recollection, excited by the recurrence of the original objects, at a period when language was little familiar: in the same manner as an animal, at a distant time brought into its former haunts, would remember the paths it had heretofore trodden.

But there are some facts in the history of recollection which do not admit of any satisfactory solution. From these it appears, that persons in their childhood have learned a language which, from the acquirement and usage of another during many years, they have entirely forgotten; so that when spoken by others, they have been wholly unable to understand it: yet during the delirium of fever, or from inflammation of the brain and its membranes, in consequence of external injury, the former and forgotten language has been revived, and spoken with fluency: but after a restoration to health no traces of its recollection have remained. A remarkable case of this kind has been published by Mr. Abernethy; and a similar instance is recorded of the lady of an ambassador. These few preliminary observations have been submitted to the reader, in order to introduce a principal part of the subject to his notice, to prevent repetitions, and from the impossibility of considering the more curious and important phenomena of perception and memory as simple and unconnected endowments.

ON THE INTELLECTUAL SUPERIORITY WHICH MAN HAS ACQUIRED BY SPEECH, AND THE POSSESSION OF THE HAND.

In our investigations of the nature and offices of the human mind, we are immediately and forcibly struck with two important circumstances, which appear to have contributed in an especial manner to the superiority of man over all other animals. Let it be admitted, without at present discussing the question, or adducing any arguments; that the constitution of the human intellect is of a higher quality, or of a finer staple, than the intelligent principle of other creatures.[2] These two endowments with which man may be considered as exclusively gifted, and which, on a deliberate survey, appear principally to have conduced to his pre-eminence in the range of intellectual creation, are speech and the possession of his hands. One of the chief characteristics by which man is distinguished from the other animals, is the capability he possesses of transmitting his acquirements to posterity. The acquirements of other animals perish with them: they are incapable of recording their achievements, and, as a community, they are stationary. If the reason be sought, it will be immediately found, that they do not enjoy the appropriate organs; and this defect will be detected to arise from their want of speech and hands.

There may perhaps arise some of the difficulties already experienced, in the separate consideration of these human attributes,—speech and the hand; as much of the superiority which man possesses has resulted from their combined assistance. It is, however, important to treat of each individually, as far as their separate influence and effects can be distinctly traced. The consideration of speech or significant sound, would naturally introduce an enquiry into its structure and philosophy: but as this knowledge can be collected from the works of many enlightened writers on these subjects, it is unnecessary to obtrude on the reader that which he may find already prepared.

Speech is *ordinarily* acquired by the ear[3], and the sound conveyed through that organ is imitated by the voice. When any object in nature is named by its appropriate articulate sound, as a tree, a fish, a horse, if the object be duly noted and the term remembered, it will mutually, on the presentation of the object, recall the term; or if the term be mentioned, the recollection of the object will arise. Without reverting to the formation of words by letters, or proceeding to the structure of sentences by words, which is the province of the grammarian, it will be seen that these significant sounds, enable human beings to convey to each other the perceptions they have experienced, or are impressed with, at the moment of communication. This endowment of speech to man would, alone, have constituted him vastly superior to the other animals. But whatever might have been his attainments, either from his own discoveries or from the experience of his contemporaries, his departure from life would have consigned the products of his genius and wisdom to the treachery and mutilation of another's recollection. Even in the enlightened and polished period of our present existence, we are fully acquainted with the loss or addition which a fact experiences, from being transmitted through a succession of narrators.

Had man been merely furnished with speech, without the means of recording his acts and reflections, we might indeed have preserved by tradition, the names of Homer, Virgil, Cicero, Shakspeare, and Milton; but their works,—those majestic columns which now support the temple of fame, would have perished, had there not been a contrivance to record the productions of their genius. This art, of conferring permanence on the significant sounds of the human voice, has taught us to appreciate and revere the taste and wisdom of our predecessors; and to feel, that although their bodies are buried in peace, yet their names live for evermore:—but more especially this contrivance has preserved the laws of nations, and above all other blessings, has transmitted, in the Sacred Volume, the commandments of the living God.

From the brief notice which has been bestowed on this subject, it will be seen, that man could have made but inconsiderable advances in the scale of intellectual progression, by speech alone;—that how much soever this faculty might have elevated him above animals, by endowing his perceptions with intelligence, and rendering his thoughts the circulating medium of his community; yet had he remained without the power of registering the edicts of his mind, language would have expired in its cradle; and as the body mingles with its mother-earth, intelligent sound would have been blended and lost in the medium that produced it.

The next subject to be considered, (and its importance will justify an ample review, and minute consideration,) is the hand; a member which may be considered, with some trifling exceptions, as exclusively bestowed on man. The wonderful construction of this part of the human body might be sufficiently exemplified by its achievements. Its anatomy has not, hitherto, been so minutely investigated, as to demonstrate the almost infinite variety of motions to which it is adapted; nor has it been sufficiently compared with the somewhat analogous structure and function in certain of the simiæ, in the claw of the parrot, or with the proboscis of the elephant.

At the extremity of the fingers, in the human hand, and on their inner surface, resides the organ of Touch; a sense, of which animals are comparatively deficient. Touch, is distinguished from feeling, which it is the general property of all the nerves to convey, and this feeling is likewise accompanied with consciousness. Thus pain may be felt in the different organs of sense, without any corresponding perception, which it is their separate office to import. Although the acute organ of touch has its seat at the extremity of the fingers, yet the whole surface of the skin (of the human subject) is susceptible, but in an inferior degree, of tangible perceptions. It is sensible of heat and cold, of hard and soft, rough and smooth. The tongue enjoys also a considerable capability of tangible discrimination; but let any person attempt to ascertain the state of his pulse, by applying the tongue to the wrist, he will find it a very unsatisfactory test.[4]

It has been already observed, that the perception of objects conveyed through the organ of vision, may be represented by drawings, so as sufficiently and accurately to convey the same perception to the eye of another: thus we recognise the likeness of a person by his portrait; the view of a known country from the landscape; the quadruped, bird, or insect, by its picture: but the perceptions of the organ of touch, can only be communicated through the medium of language; and the same may be observed concerning those derived from the smell and taste. We may indeed submit the same objects of touch, smell, and taste, to a number of persons, who, in all probability, (their organs being similar,) would be impressed with the same perceptions: but these perceptions, recollected, and the objects which excited them absent, can only be communicated through the medium of significant sound.

It may be a subject of curious investigation, although foreign to our present enquiry, whether man, in possession of articulate organs, discovered speech, and imposed names on his perceptions; or whether he was originally gifted with this endowment. Without attempting to discuss this question, it is sufficient to remark, that the structure and composition of our own language, and of its northern kindred, afford sufficient evidence of a very rude and necessitous origin.

After man had acquired the means of communicating his perceptions by significant sounds, the next important discovery was the art of recording them, so that they might serve as the vehicle of intelligence to his distant contemporaries, or be transmitted to posterity as the sources of improvement. The human hand is the immediate agent by which this contrivance is displayed. It is not intended to trace the history of this wonderful and precious discovery, but to remark, that human ingenuity, has likewise established the record of sounds which are not significant, and which are termed the notations of music.

The science of accurate admeasurements has been exclusively discovered by man; and for the attainment of this important acquisition, it will be seen that the hand has been chiefly and progressively instrumental. When we contemplate the present state of man, in our own nation, surrounded by the conveniences which gratify his wants, and behold him practised in their enjoyment, we are little disposed to revert to that period of his history, when he struggled to continue his existence, and trace his tardy progression from rudeness to refinement.

Pleas'd with himself, the coxcomb rears his head,

And scorns the dunghill where he first was bred.

Although we now measure space and time, bodies solid and fluid, heat and its absence with the facility of a single glance; yet if we consider the slow, and painful steps, by which such acquirements have been attained, we shall be forcibly impressed, how much we are the creatures of patient experiment, and also how mainly the hand has contributed to our advancement. If we investigate the standards of admeasurement, we find that many have been derived from the human body, and more especially from its operative instrument, the hand. That the members and dimensions of our own body should have been the original standards of measurement is most natural, and the terms in which they are conveyed afford a sufficient illustration of the fact. Thus, we have a nail; *pollex, pouce, pulgada,* Swedish *tum,* for an inch; which word has been misapplied by our Saxon predecessors, and corrupted from the Latin *uncia,* which related only to weight. We still measure by digits, by fingers' breadth, by hands high. Cubit from *cubitus,* was formerly employed. We now retain ell, *aune, ulna.* Foot, pace, *pas, pes.* Yard, not as Mr. Tooke supposed from the Saxon gyrwan, to prepare, but from gyrdan, *cingere,* and is employed to represent the girth of the body. Fathom, the distance of the arms when extended to embrace, from which the meaning is implied in most languages.[5] But it will be immediately perceived, that measurement could not proceed to any considerable extent, could neither be compounded by addition, nor subdivided, without the employment and comprehension of numbers.

In our childhood we are taught the knowledge of numbers; and those who have superintended the work of education, must have witnessed the difficulty of impressing on the mind of the child, this kind of information. Alphabetic characters, compared with numbers, are readily acquired: whether it be from the imperfect manner, in which the science of numbers is usually taught, or from the actual difficulty in comprehending the subject, it is not pretended to determine; although, from some considerations, the latter is most probable. The names of different objects are easily acquired, and children examine such objects by their different senses, more especially by the eye and touch; they become desirous of learning their properties, or of becoming acquainted with their construction: and this investigation affords them delight, and excites or gratifies their curiosity. But numbers possess no such attraction; numbers, do not involve any of the obvious properties of these objects, neither their colour, shape, sound, smell, or taste; it therefore becomes perplexing for them to comprehend, if five similar substances, as so many apples, or nuts, be arranged before them, why each, should bear a name, different from the thing itself, and different from each other: why this nut should be termed one, another two, and the next three.

In acquiring a knowledge of numbers, as far as the senses are concerned, the eye and the touch are especially exercised; but it appears that the touch is the corrector of the sight: if fifty pieces of money be laid on a table, they will sooner and more accurately be numbered by the touch, than the eye; and we know in other instances, that the motion of the hand is quicker than the discernment of the sight. There are many circumstances, although they do not amount to a proof, which might induce us to consider, that the human hand has much contributed to our knowledge of numbers.[6]

As far as we possess any direct evidence, none of the animals are capable of numerating; and this constitutes an essential difference between them and man in their intellectual capacities. In states of weakness of mind, this defect in the power of numerating, is very observable, and forms a just and admitted criterion of idiotcy; and it is well known that such persons exercise the organ of touch in a very limited degree, compared with those of vigorous capacity: their fingers are likewise more taper, and their sentient extremities less pulpy and expanded. The same state of the organ of touch may be remarked in some lunatics who have become idiotic, or where the hands have been confined for a considerable time.

Although in our own language, we have not been able to discover any rational etymology of the units, that is, what was originally the meaning of one, two, three, &c., or of what these units were the representatives, we have, however, by the ingenuity of Mr. Tooke, a very probable account of the origin of ten, which means, that which includes, or comprehends all numeration; and that it does so include it, may be learned from the composition of eleven[7]; and if it should amount to no more than a curious coincidence, ten is the number of the manual extremities. Notwithstanding neither our own, nor any of the European tongues, afford us any probable solution of the actual meaning or import of the units, yet this contrivance is satisfactorily developed in the language of some of the African tribes, (vide Park's Travels, p. 337.) where it will be found, that when they had arrived at six, they proceeded by composition; not by the composition of six and one, to form seven, but by five and two.

One—*Kidding.*

Two—*Fidding.*

Three—*Sarra.*

Four—*Nani.*

Five—*Soolo.*

Six—*Seni.*

Seven—*Soolo ma Fidding*—Five and Two.

Eight—*Soolo ma Sarra*—Five and Three.

Nine—*Soolo ma Nani*—Five and Four.

Ten—*Nuff.*

As numbers must have been acquired in progression,—first one, then two, &c. there appears to be considerable difficulty in conceiving, of what the increase or addition would be the representative, except by adding the already designated numbers together: but our own units do not bear any ostensible marks of such composition, nor do the northern numerals, from whence our own have been imported. If we were now called on to construct a new language, and invent terms for the units, there are no objects familiar to me, which would suggest appropriate terms, as the types of the different units; and it is presumed, as far as we have extended our researches, that the names of things are not arbitrary, but have been imposed for some real or supposed reason.

When we consider the importance of numbers to man, as an intellectual being, and compare the advancement he has made by this knowledge, beyond the animals who have wanted the means of acquiring such information, the importance of investigating this curious subject will be fully acknowledged. Without numbers, by which the divisions of time, space, and value are characterised, man could have possessed no knowledge of the order and succession of events; he would, by wanting precise standards, have remained ignorant of admeasurements; and without the definite proportions which numbers confer, property would be a vague and uncertain name.

From these remarks an opportunity is now presented, to enumerate the important achievements of the human hand; but as a powerful objection may be urged, against the views which have been sketched out concerning this subject, it will be proper to notice them, in order to refer their discussion to another and more appropriate chapter. It will naturally be stated that the hand is the mere auxiliary, in fact, the servant, of the mind; and in a healthy state of intellect is regulated by its directions, in the performances it executes. The truth of this, it is not intended to deny; but the examination of the objection must be referred to that part of the work, which treats of the influence, which does so regulate and direct, namely, the will, or, as it has been more scholastically termed, volition.

We readily acknowledge that he who is born blind can have no perception of visible objects, and that the same negation may be extended to the other senses when defective: thus, if man had been created without hands, and, consequently, without the acute organ of touch, which resides in the extremities of these members, we must at least have been strangers to the "cloud-capt towers, the gorgeous palaces, and the solemn temples" which he has reared. Had the upper extremities of the human body terminated at the wrist, such a man as Phidias might have existed, but his occupation would have been unknown. Thus truncated, how would the fleet have been constructed which reaped the laurel at the Nile, at Copenhagen, and Trafalgar? The eternal city could not have existed, nor would our own metropolis have had a being. If we reflect for an instant, we shall perceive that all the conveniences we enjoy, all the arts we practise, and the sciences which elevate and dignify our nature, could never have been realised in a handless community. Speech might indeed have prevailed, but its record could not have been established, and intelligent sounds would only have served to breathe forth the lamentations of misery and despair, or the accents of discontent. We must have remained naked, and perished from the inclemency of weather: man would have owed "the worm no silk, the beast no hide, the sheep no wool." It would be superfluous to pursue this subject further, as the reader has only to consider the superior enjoyments, and accumulated monuments, of art and of wisdom, which the mind of man has produced by the agency of his hand.

"Molto opró egli col senno ed con la mano."

However it may gratify the pride of man, to find himself gifted with intellectual endowments of a higher order, and distinguished as the lord of creation; yet he must, on reflection, regard this superiority as a "painful pre-eminence." The possession of speech, and hands, the prompt executors of his will, have enabled him to become the perpetrator of crimes to which the tribes of animals are strangers. Language has exclusively furnished man with the means of promulgating the result of his perceptions and thoughts: he thereby becomes capable of communicating to others, that which he has observed, or the opinions he has formed; and so highly has this accuracy of relation been estimated, in all periods of civilised society, that it has been proudly denominated the truth. But the possession of the same faculty of speech, has often induced him to relate that which never occurred, or to disown that which actually took place; and this assertion or denial has been severely reprobated and stigmatised by the appellation of a lie. It is unnecessary to enumerate the catalogue of the articulate vices which the tongue can commit, or sully the dignity of human nature, by the recollection that its lord has been convicted of perjury, slander, blasphemy, and libel. Thus, the hand, this admirable instrument, the elaborations of which excite our wonder and delight, whether we contemplate the chiselled monuments of Grecian art, or the curious manufactures of modern days,—all that is tasteful in art, or auxiliary to science,—even this plastic and creative member, the faithful notary of thought,— becomes the prostituted engine of the vilest fraud, or foulest atrocity. The same hand that fashioned the Minerva of the Parthenon might have picked a lock, or directed a dagger. It will be found, on an accurate investigation, that all laws, which are the VOICE of those whom we have delegated, or who may have assumed such power, and which are recorded by the hand, are principally directed to the lesions against individuals or society, which proceed from speech, or are perpetrated by the hand.

FOOTNOTES:

[2] It must be felt by the reader that all the epithets, which can be applied to designate this superiority, must be of material character and signification:—whether we say superior structure, texture, purity, &c. In fact, we possess no

appropriate expressions, to characterise that which is not material: but this poverty of language, affords no ground for the materiality of mind; on the contrary, it is a strong argument against such doctrine, that we are obliged to clothe the phenomena of mind in the garb of metaphor; for material objects can be well defined according to their obvious properties.

[3] Those who are born deaf are taught to imitate articulate sounds independently of the ear.

[4] The reader may refer to works on comparative anatomy, for information concerning this sense in animals. They all agree that no animal possesses a complete hand, and that the thumb is especially defective in size, and in the strength which enables it to act in opposition to the combined force of the fingers. The sense of touch in many animals appears to reside in the large and fleshy nostrils, which appear highly sensible; and it is also evident, that in these the touch has an intimate alliance with their sense of smell.

[5] It is equally curious to observe that geographical positions, and the principal features of sea and land, have derived their origin from the rude anatomy of the human body. Thus, in a short enumeration we have cape or *head*-land, ness, noss, or *nose*; the *brow* of a mountain; *tongue* of land; *mouth* of a river; *chaps* of the channel; *neck* of land; *arm* of the sea; coast, *costæ*, the ribs. We are said to penetrate into the *heart* of the country, or to remove to the *back* settlements. We descend into the *bowels* of the earth, in order to discover a *vein* of ore. We ascend from the *foot* of the mountain; and from its *ridge* (back) survey the prospect surrounding. Numerous additions might be contributed by further recollection.

[6] On many occasions we observe the hands to be the natural refuge for the destitute in arithmetic, and therefore are not surprised at finding many persons counting by their fingers. Some rude nations are said not to have advanced in their numeration beyond five: this may perhaps be uncertain and difficult to prove; but it will be shewn that when others have advanced to ten, that seven has been the compound of five and two, eight of five and three, &c.

[7] It is not uninteresting to examine the contrivances that have been resorted to, in order to express the number eleven. The Greeks had ενδεχα [Greek: *endeka*], one (and subaudit) ten; the Romans *undecem*; and a similar adoption has been employed by the southern nations of Europe. The northern people expressed eleven, by *one left* (after ten, subaudit.) thus Caxton states his Recuyels of Troy to have been "ended and fynished in the holy cyte of Colen, the 19th day of Septembre, in the yere of our sayd Lord God, a thousand four hundred sixty and *enleven*." *En*, in old English, means one, and *leven* is the past participle of, to leave, formerly written leve.

ON THE NATURE AND COMPOSITION OF LANGUAGE, AS APPLIED TO THE INVESTIGATION OF THE PHENOMENA OF MIND.

Mind, is an abstract term for all the phenomena of intelligence; and in order to describe them, they have usually been denominated powers, or faculties of the mind: we therefore commonly speak concerning the mind, as of an existence endowed with these properties.[8] It has been already confessed, that we are at present uninformed, and in all probability shall remain ignorant of the nature and operation of our intellectual powers: at least, we shall never be able to comprehend the manner in which we perceive the objects that surround us, nor to explain how we recollect them when they are absent; yet under this acknowledged inability we have framed a language expressive of these powers and operations. This language therefore cannot be the type of such processes, as their nature and operation are unknown. The different terms that have been employed, have originated from the numerous hypotheses, which have prevailed on this subject: but so long as a perfect agreement subsists, concerning the meaning of these terms, it is of little importance; for as we have no knowledge of the actual processes, whereby we perceive, remember, or exert our will, the expressions we employ cannot be explanatory. The language of mind, therefore, is not peculiar, not derived as the nomenclature of modern chemistry, in which names are impregnated with the elements of their composition; but figurative or metaphorical, the vehicle of conjecture, and the ornament of hypothesis.

The truth of these remarks, would be best illustrated by an enumeration and analysis of the terms, which have been applied, to designate the powers and operations of the human intellect.

Were we now to occupy ourselves, in the construction of a more appropriate language, to designate and explain the phenomena of mind; we should, from our ignorance, be equally incompetent with those who have preceded us. Let the terms therefore remain, but endeavour to afford them a fixed and definite meaning, and suffer them to be so far analysed, as to detect their composition, and discover the reasons which imposed them. In this endeavour there will, however, be found considerable difficulty; especially as the minds of men are not yet agreed respecting the process, by which it is to be performed.

There are, however, only two modes, to which we can resort, for the definite meaning of words; namely, etymology and authority. Considering the history of our own language, and the nature of its composition, we are enabled satisfactorily to investigate, not only the primitive sense of our terms, but likewise their exact signification, in the languages from whence we imported them: for there still remain, sufficient authentic materials, in our Saxon and Norman records, to verify their original meaning. If we enquire into the causes, which have operated to deflect these terms from their primitive sense, we shall find authority to be the principal source of such corruption; and this infirmity appears to have pervaded most of the languages of those nations which have produced poets, orators, and metaphysicians.[9] When we examine the nature of authority in language, as it now exists, we find it to be the arbitrary employment of words, by particular writers of acknowledged celebrity. Many have become authorities in our language, from having improved its construction; others, by the perspicuous arrangement of subject, by the force of their reasoning, or the light of their philosophy. Although we may allow the highest merit to these eminent writers, a praise, far beyond the dulness and drudgery of verbal criticism; yet it is by no means to be inferred, that they consequently become authorities, for the real and intrinsic meaning of words. It can never be expected, that the great mass of mankind should be etymologists: the generality must be regulated by the "jus et norma loquendi;" but if this jus, be the jus vagum, and the norma capricious, confusion must ensue, and they will scarcely be speaking the same language. Those who are dignified with the title of authorities, ought to agree; for the sound interpreters of the law should never differ.

Language is the circulating medium of our thoughts; and the meaning of words much resembles the value of money. But great diversity of opinion prevails. In the minds of some philosophers, money means only metallic currency, which may be assayed, and its real value ascertained; and this seems to relate to etymology. Others less solid in their views, and gifted with a finer fabric of fancy, are disposed to consider the abstractions of paper to be equivalent to the concrete of bullion, and have accordingly constituted it the jus and norma by authority. To insist on the meaning of a word, because its interpretation has been previously assumed, carries no conviction of its truth. The "jus et norma loquendi," must ever prevail as the currency between human beings; but this acknowledgment should not, in the course of circulation, diminish, the undoubted right we possess, to detect and refuse such as are base or counterfeit.

It will not be disputed, that some words bear a much higher importance than others. The names of familiar objects are of little consequence, because we can examine them by our senses, and thereby obtain just perceptions of their character and properties: but general or abstract terms, which are not the objects of sense, but the abbreviations of subjects of reflection, are of the highest interest to our advancement in knowledge and moral conduct. To exemplify the views that have been taken on this subject, three words have been selected:—*to feel, to ransack,* and the adjective, *naked.* Of the first, Dr. Johnson, the best authority we now possess, has given six different senses or acceptations as a verb active, and four, as a verb neuter, and has cited the different authorities.

He says it is derived from the Anglo-Saxon, *felan*, without explaining what *felan* means; it however means to feel: but the adduction of a word in another language, of similar sound and identical signification, does not impart meaning. Yet when we find that in the Anglo-Saxon *fell* means *skin*, which is the seat of feeling, we directly understand the word and all its dependencies; as *fell* of hair, *felt* hat, *fell*-monger, *film*, which is a thin fine skin or pellicle. Thus we become enabled to understand and reconcile variety and extension of meaning, from the preservation of integrity of figure.

The verb *to ransack*, is another example. Of this word Dr. Johnson has given three senses. According to him, it is derived from *ran*, Anglo-Saxon, and *saka*, Swedish, to search or seize; but we are not informed what *ran* in Anglo-Saxon signifies, and it so happens that there is no such Swedish word as *saka*, to search. The word *ransack*, for which the Anglo-Saxons had *ransaka*, is derived to us from the Gothic, in which *razn* (pronounced *ran*) signifies a house, and *sokjan* to search; so that, *to ransack*, implies to search the house.

To the adjective *naked* Dr. Johnson has given four different meanings. Its etymology, he says, is from the Anglo-Saxon, *nacod*, which in that language was of similar signification: but this imparts no meaning. It is a compound word: *na*, in Anglo-Saxon, signifies *new*, and *cenned*, *born*, so that the condition of the *new-born* child affords an appropriate interpretation of the term *naked*.

To ordinary minds, that which is said to be authority is decisive[10]; a particular author of celebrity is cited, and thus the business concludes. The reasons, which induced him to employ the word in such particular sense, it is in most cases fruitless to enquire; as during their lives, authors have seldom

29

been appreciated: so that the silence of death seems indispensable to procure the consent of authority.

As language is the instrument of thought, the vehicle of intelligible communication among human beings, it is impossible to attach too high importance to its precise signification: the difficulties of effecting this concordance have been pointed out, but the remedy has not yet been applied. After all the investigation that has been given to this interesting subject, one leading fact seems indisputable, that all the terms which designate the faculties and operations of our minds, are of physical origin, as well as those which characterise the thinking or immaterial principle itself: and for this, there is sufficient reason; as all language, in order to be adapted for our use, in this state of existence, can only be the representative of the objects of our perceptions and reflections,—an instrument calculated for the meridian of this transitory life: for, when the holy light of happiness to come was revealed to the human race, it was found expedient, for their comprehension, to transmit its rays through a material prism.[11]

FOOTNOTES:

[8] Mr. Locke, as he advances in his essay, expresses considerable distrust of the existence of these powers and faculties of the mind. "Yet I suspect, I say, that this way of speaking of faculties has misled many into a confused notion of so many distinct agents in us, which had their several provinces and authorities, and did command, obey, and perform several actions, as so many distinct beings; which has been no small occasion of wrangling, obscurity, and uncertainty in questions relating to them."—Vol. i. p. 192. 10th edition.

[9] To afford a single illustration of this fact, let the verb to *bewray* be selected, which, although a word of very different meaning, has been confounded with to *betray*. The meaning of the former is to discover, expose, and is derived from a Saxon verb bearing that sense; the latter, Dr. Johnson has derived from the French *trahir*, and has cited some instances, as authorities for its perverted sense. It is but justice to observe, that these words preserve their distinct and separate sense in all the instances where they have been employed, both in Shakspeare and the Bible. It may therefore be inferred, to have been a recent corruption.

[10] Of this, Mr. Locke appears to have been fully sensible:— "When men are established in any kind of dignity, 'tis thought a breach of modesty for others to derogate any way from it, and question the authority of men who are in possession of it. This is apt to be censured, as carrying with it too much of pride, when a man does not readily yield to the determination of approved authors, which is wont to be received with respect and submission by others; and 'tis looked upon as insolence for a man to set up, and adhere to his own opinion, against the current stream of antiquity, or to put in the balance against that of some learned doctor, or otherwise approved writer. Whoever backs his tenets with such authorities, thinks he ought thereby to carry the cause; and is ready to stile it impudence in any one who shall stand out against them."—Locke's Works, vol. ii. p. 306.

[11] This material prism is to be understood to apply to language; and in this view Newton himself surveyed the question. "For all language as applied to God, is taken from the affairs of men, by some resemblance, not indeed a perfect one, but yet existing to a certain degree."—Newton's Works, edit. Horsley, vol. iv. p. 430.

31

ON WILL OR VOLITION.

In the consideration of the nature and offices of the human mind, there is no subject of higher importance than the will, or volition. Every person must have observed, that he is capable of performing certain motions, which he is able to commence, to continue, and to arrest; and the same faculty is possessed by many animals. A slight degree of information will also instruct him, that there are certain motions of his animal frame, over which he has no immediate control. The motions which he is able to direct and regulate, have been termed voluntary; and those over which he possesses no influence or command, have been denominated involuntary motions. The most perfect instances of the latter are the pulsations of the heart, and the movements of the intestines, usually called peristaltic. The curiosity which is natural to man as an intelligent being, would of course prompt him to enquire into the cause of these phenomena, although the result of his investigations might be inadequate to the toil of his research: for, he would be as much puzzled to account for the influence by which certain muscles are moved at will, as he would at others which possess a determinate motion, and are not subject to this direction. While man continues in a healthy state, he is enabled to move at pleasure those muscles or instruments of motion which are subject to his will; and the involuntary muscles continue duly to perform their appropriate office; but in certain morbid states it sometimes occurs, that the exertion of the will to move a leg or arm is ineffectually directed, and however much we desire, wish, or will such motion, these limbs are disobedient.[12] This condition of the members has been termed paralytic: the will to move remains perfect; but the organs to be acted on are insensible to that influence which, in a sound state, excited them to motion. As in the healthy state the will has the power to produce motion, so it is also competent to prevent it; therefore to move or to abstain from motion, are equally the dictates of the will. But it not unfrequently happens, when we intend to thread a needle, to write our name, or to perform some surgical operation, that the will exerts all its influence to keep the hand steady for the due performance of these necessary acts; yet, notwithstanding these implicit commands, the hand continues to move in all directions, but those which could accomplish the object. So, that these muscles, ordinarily voluntary, become, in a certain degree, converted into involuntary muscles. A higher degree of this state prevails in the affection called St. Vitus' Dance, and likewise in some convulsive symptoms attendant on locked jaw, where the body is drawn with incredible violence. It may be noticed, that these states are attended with consciousness.

Concerning the nature of this influence, termed the *will*, a great variety of discordant opinions prevail. To enumerate or refute these would be unprofitable labour, more especially as the majority are the mere assumptions of their particular authors. They all, however, seem to be agreed that the will is an inherent faculty, or component part of the mind; and some are induced to consider it as holding the highest office in the department of intellect. The only mode of investigating this subject satisfactorily, according to my own views, is to trace the progress of volition from its feeble commencement, to the full exercise of its important function,—from the dawn to the meridian.

As a general observation, it may be remarked that the same influence of the will, which directs the movements of the body, is likewise exerted over the faculties of the mind; although generally in an inferior degree, both from the greater difficulty and less importance of the latter, for the ordinary purposes of life. When we observe the newly-born infant,—that helpless mass of animation,—we perceive no indications to induce us to conclude, that it possesses a voluntary power of directing its movements.[13] It is furnished with the organs of motion, but is unable to exert that influence which manifests direction; yet its involuntary motions continue perfect, and these, as will be subsequently explained, may be considered in their nature and effects as very similar to that, which, in animals, is termed instinct. In the progress of this enquiry, it will be seen that some degree of mental advancement must have been made, before the infant can *direct* any of the motions of its body; because direction implies knowledge to an extent sufficient for the purposes of command, and also a consciousness of the effort. In the infant, all the organs of sense by degrees become awaked by their appropriate stimuli or objects, and perception is the result. Although we have no memory of our earliest perceptions, which are solely produced by the excitation of external objects, without any direction of the will; yet from the mental indications of the infant, these perceptions would seem to be confused and indistinct. It is some time before the eye appears to notice, and longer before the hand can grasp and manipulate the substances within its reach: in this state, volition would be superfluous if it were possessed. By slow gradations, we find the child capable of directing its eye, of listening to sounds, and of examining by the touch; and these imply the efforts of the will, which appear to be subsequent to perception. As we advance in knowledge, our perceptions, which are the sources of intelligence, are principally acquired by the agency of volition, which directs the organ to the object, but we still continue to be acted on involuntarily by forcible impressions, or striking phenomena.

Previously to the acquirement of language, perception, memory, and volition are in their simplest state, such as we observe in animals, and as in them, we are only able to estimate the amount of their mental possessions, from the intellectual phenomena they display. In the infant, the separate and combined examination of objects by the eye and touch are the circumstances most deserving of notice.

It may here be proper to explain why these earliest of our perceptions are never remembered in after-life. The long period of human infancy, is a powerful argument for the superiority of our species: the mind of man is built up by his own exertions, and his progress is in the ratio of his experience to his capacity: his mission is more important, and consequently requires a longer period to fulfil: he has few instincts; and the sum of his knowledge is the elaboration of his extended endowments. To have remembered the confused dawnings of his perceptions, the imperfect and obscure transmissions of his unpractised organs would have been superfluous, and the sources of error. In this early state, there is no medium by which his perceptions can be artificially connected; nor do they admit of communication or record. When language is acquired, our perceptions become "doubly armed," and impress the memory with additional effect: the employment of the term as the representative of the object, recalls the original perception, and thus invests the mental phantasm with "a local habitation and a name." Thus our earliest recollections are never anterior to a certain progress in the art of speech.

As we possess the instruments of motion in our muscles, they would have been useless without the performance of their function, and our bodies would have been stationary. It is also equally evident that this office must be performed by ourselves, or fulfilled by others. It has been already pointed out that there are certain motions, essential to the preservation of our animal system, termed *involuntary*, which do not originate from ourselves, but are the directions of a superior power, and are effected independently of our experience and control: the other motions, that have been termed voluntary, are the result of acquirement or practice, and have been gradually formed by our exertions. The reader will now be prepared to understand the wisdom of this arrangement, which, in a future chapter, will be more copiously treated; and to feel that the superiority of man, as an intellectual being, and a responsible agent, consists in the formation of his own mind, and in the direction of his thoughts and actions.

That we should exert our utmost endeavours to become acquainted with the nature of this influence, which we term the will, is most natural; but hitherto our researches have been wholly unavailing; and it should be recollected that the appearances of life cannot be accounted for by that which is inanimate, nor can the phenomena of intelligence be solved by material analogies. As we are possessed of the implements of motion, it is evident that they were constructed to accomplish their destined purpose; but of the intimate nature of the stimulus which goads them to action, we have no conception: it seems, however, certain that there exists a mutual consent,—a reciprocal subaudition,—a compact, the result of exercise and experience,—between the implements of motion and the will or influence which excites them.

As far as we are able to discover, by the most attentive and deliberate examination of our own minds, we do not appear conscious of any intermediate perception, between the motive and the performance of the action, or the execution of the will. If it were allowable to indulge in analogical reasoning, which usually diverts us from the consideration of the subject, we might endeavour to illustrate this process by the firing of a pistol. When we have taken due aim, we have only to draw the trigger, which produces the explosion: in doing this, however, we perceive the emission of light from the combustion of the powder; but to this there is nothing analogous in the operation of the will:—the dictate of the will, and the motion excited, when watched with the utmost attention, appear instantaneous, and become synchronous by habit. Considering the celerity of our voluntary movements, there appears a good reason why no perceptible intervention should exist, to divert the mind from the immediate performance of the will. The correspondence of the motion to the intimation of the will, is the business of education and the performance of habit.

The exertion of the will on the bodily organs having been generally described, it now remains to demonstrate its influence on the mind; and so far as we are enabled to discover, it appears to be performed by the same process. The direction of the several organs of sense to the examination of objects, is an act of the will, and has been named Attention; which, by some writers, has been deemed a peculiar and constituent faculty of the mind; but in the present view it is considered only as the practical result of the operation of volition on the organs of sense, on memory, and on reflection. The soundest mind (as far as it has been hitherto considered) may be attributed to him who possesses the most enduring control over the organs of sense, in order to examine objects accurately, and thereby to acquire a full and complete perception. That memory is the best, which can voluntarily and immediately produce that which has been committed to its custody; and that reflection is the most perfect, which is exclusively occupied with the subject of consideration. There seems also to be a considerable similarity between the morbid states of the instruments of voluntary motion, and certain affections of the mental powers: thus, paralysis has its counterpart in the defects of recollection, where the utmost endeavour to remember is ineffectually exerted; tremor may be compared with incapability of fixing the attention, and this involuntary state of muscles ordinarily subjected to the will, also finds a parallel, where the mind loses its influence on the train of thought, and becomes subject to spontaneous intrusions; as may be exemplified in reverie, dreaming, and some species of madness.

As attention is considered an exertion of the will on the organs of sense and faculties of the mind, it may be allowable to remark on the nature and meaning of the term. It was evidently imposed under a prevailing hypothesis, that the mind possessed a power of stretching or extending itself to the objects of its perception, or to the subjects of reflection; it is therefore a figurative term. Indeed something of this nature actually takes place in the organ:—in minute examinations by the eye, we actually strain and stretch its muscles, and feel the fatigue which results from over-exertion:—when we listen, the neck is stretched forward, and such position enables us to collect those vibrations of sound, that would be otherwise inaudible. We are not unaccustomed to describe the higher and more felicitous productions of intellect, as a vigorous grasp of the mental powers, or as a noble stretch of thought: but to infer that the mind itself was capable of being extended, would be to invest it directly with the properties of substance, and at once plunge us into the grossest materialism. The perfection of this voluntary direction, or, as it has been termed, faculty of attention, consists in intensity and duration. Of the former there can be no admeasurement, excepting by its effect, which is recollection: its duration can be well ascertained. The faculty of attention in the human mind may be exerted in two ways; first, by the organs of sense to the objects of perception; and, secondly, by the mind to the subjects of its recollection; and this latter exercise of attention, as will be hereafter explained, seems to be in a very great degree peculiar to man, and to be nearly wanting in animals.

According to the nature and constitution of the human mind, the effective duration of the attention seems to be very limited: if the eye be steadily directed to any particular object, after a few seconds, it will be found to wander; and if the mind be exerted on the subjects of its recollection, there is very soon perceived an interruption, from the intrusion of irrelevant thoughts. The effective duration of the attention will much depend on the superior capacity, nature, or constitution of the intellect itself; but still more on the manner in which these habits of attention are exercised; for, by proper cultivation, its duration may be considerably protracted. As a proof of the limited endurance of the faculty of attention in ordinary minds, allow the following experiment to be made.

Let two ordinary persons, A. and B., take a map of a district with which they are unacquainted, and let each be allowed half an hour to study the map. Desire A. to fix his attention undeviatingly to the map for this time; and at its expiration, the map being withdrawn, request him to put on paper the relative situations and names of the different places; and for the performance of his task, allow him another half hour. As the experiment has been repeatedly made, it may be confidently predicted, that A. would exhibit a very incorrect copy of the original map. Let B. take the same map to study for the same time; but instead of keeping his eyes undeviatingly fixed to the object, desire him to view it only for a few seconds; and then, shutting his eyes, let him endeavour to bring the picture of the map before his mind: his first efforts will convey a very confused notion of the actual and relative positions; but he will become sensible of his defects, and reinspect the map for their correction. If this successive ocular examination and review by the mind, be continued during the half hour, or even for a less time, B. will be competent to make a drawing of the map with superior accuracy to A., who endeavoured to fix his attention for the whole of the time allotted. In conducting this experiment some very curious phenomena may be observed. If A. had directed his eyes to the object intensely and undeviatingly, especially in a strong light, and had then covered or shut his eyes, in order to recollect the relative situations in the map, the straining of the organ to the object would defeat his endeavours; and instead of being able to bring the picture before his mind, he would be annoyed and interrupted by the intrusion of ocular spectra, undergoing the succession of changes described by Dr. Darwin.[14] Thus there are limits to the duration of our effective attention: if the organ of vision be too long directed to the object of perception, ocular spectra arise, fatigue and confusion ensue in the other senses; and if the subjects of recollection be too long and intensely contemplated, delirium will supervene.

40

In page 52, after enumerating the wonderful productions of the hand, an objection was foreseen, which may be conveniently examined in the present chapter. That all the performances of the human hand, and of the other members of the body, which are not the result of involuntary movements, must have been the consequence of the direction of the will, is indisputable: it is, in fact, the common relation of cause and effect: but the creation of this distinction, would assign separate offices to the mind and to the organ;—or to the power directing, and to the instrument by which the command is executed. Sufficient has been already adduced, to render it obvious, that mind or organ *alone* would be inadequate for the purposes of intelligence. Perception, without its record or memory, would be a useless endowment; muscles or organs of motion, without a power to direct their actions, could have answered no purpose: to be effective, volition must have an object on which its influence can be exerted. In the case of a paralytic arm or leg, the exercise of the will is a fruitless endeavour; and the command to render fixed a tremulous hand is equally unavailing. The power or capacity of moving the muscles,—of directing the organs of sense to the examination of objects,—of recollecting,—and of regulating our thoughts or reflections, constitutes the will; but this acquirement is of very gradual formation, and the result of mutual and progressive exercise, both of mind and organ. Ordinary persons have no information of the structure by which they perform their motions; and it may be also doubted if an able anatomist would be competent to describe the action of the different muscles, in complicated movements. The most dexterous artificer, is wholly ignorant of the intimate construction of the organs by which he performs his wonderful elaborations,—he has acquired the happy facility by repeated exercise. There is

41

a tacit and practical convention between his mind and the powers which produce the performance; tacit, as he is unable to describe them, and practical, as, if naturally left-handed, he is unable by any mental directions or influence of volition, to exhibit the same performance with the right. The apparent facility and astonishing rapidity with which, by practice, we perform many of our voluntary motions, has induced an opinion, that such motions might be considered as automatical, which implies that they were performed by the organ independently of the will; but this would be to maintain, that the most difficult and felicitous of our voluntary motions were themselves involuntary. This supposition is so absurd that it refutes itself; its admission would be a libel on the perfection of human attainment, and tend to subvert the best portion of our existing morality.

That voluntary muscles may be converted into involuntary, has been already observed; but this conversion is to be considered a morbid state, and must be regarded as a degradation of our nature, instead of its perfection. Excess in the use of fermented liquors, will generally produce it; and the habitual practice of intemperance will destroy the influence of volition over the intellectual powers; so that the control over the succession of our thoughts can be no longer exerted, and when we give them utterance they are without connection, and we talk at random.

It is not to be expected, in a work which professes to be merely contributions to the Natural History and Physiology of Intelligent Beings, that a particular discussion of moral subjects should be instituted; and such is the question concerning the freedom of the human will: the reader is therefore referred to those writers who have fully, and with considerable acuteness, discussed this intricate and important topic. The nature of this attribute is however so interwoven with the philosophy of mind, so connected with the view which has been taken of its history and constitution, that it is impossible wholly to abstain from the consideration of its influence on the excellence and demerit of human actions. It has been endeavoured, throughout this chapter, to establish, that the power which goads or stimulates the muscles to action, and the mind to exertion, is not inherent, but acquired by practice; and this is exemplified by the state of the new-born infant, which, at that period, manifests no more of volition, than of perception, reflection, or reason. It has also been conjectured, that the possession of this influence must be subsequent to perception, for reasons which have been assigned. With its intimate nature we are unacquainted; but we see, as far as muscular motion is concerned, that the same effect is produced by the stimulus of galvanism after the head is removed, and when, according to our existing philosophy, consciousness is destroyed, and the power of willing is abolished. It is by no means intended to suppose that the stimulus of the will has any affinity with the galvanic fluid, because we are unable to prove it; although such opinion has been entertained. According to my own interpretation, Will is to be considered as the mere spur, the simple stimulus to action: it possesses no intelligence to direct; but in the healthy state, excites motion in consequence of being itself directed to such excitement. To invest Will with intelligence sufficient for its purposes, would render reason, the highest of our attainments, superfluous. Those who have most strenuously contended for the freedom of the will, have insisted that it possesses the liberty of choosing or preferring: allow this, and then enquire what must be the nature of that choice or preference, which is selected by an arbitrary decision, without the previous estimate or calculation of reason. Man, beyond all other beings, is endowed with superior means of accumulating knowledge, and of preserving experience; by these, therefore, his actions should be directed. If, independently of these, his will possessed a power of directing his actions, it would be equivalent to the instinct of animals: he would, like them, be stationary, and his conduct liable to no responsibility. The long period of infancy in man has been frequently adverted to; and it is a considerable time before he acquires sufficient experience to direct his conduct; and during which, many of the species of animals have completed several generations. For this reason, the wisest legislators, of all ages, have exempted children under a certain age, from the punishment of death for their actions; and although many of them have entertained erroneous notions concerning the nature of the will, yet they tacitly admit, in the instances of infants, idiots, and madmen,—that is, where the understanding is not sufficiently formed by experience, or where it is perverted by disease, that the acts of the will ought not to be visited by the severity of the law. This is perhaps the best practical illustration, that the will to act, is governed and directed by reason. Had the mind of man, like animals, been furnished with instinct, which, in them, implies a wise, preconcerted, and unvarying performance of important functions, for their individual preservation, and for the continuance of their race,—as may be exemplified in the construction of the habitations of the bee and beaver, together with their wonderful economy,—the fabrication of the spider's web, and many others,—he would, like them, have been stationary, having received from Infinite Bounty and Wisdom sufficient for his destination: his will would have been directed by unerring motives; and thus his conduct would have been absolved from all responsibility. But man is gifted

44

with few instincts, which appear to decline as his reason advances: his intellect is more capacious, and of a finer staple; he possesses additional organs for the accumulation of knowledge; and, by the peculiarity of his construction, is enabled to preserve his acquirements, to avail himself of the treasures of those who have preceded him, and to transmit his collections to posterity. Man, in possession of ampler materials and superior capacity, becomes the architect of his own mind; and to him it is alone permitted, by the aid of experience, and the estimate of reason, to direct his actions: but this generous and exalted faculty involves him in awful responsibility. The same light which discovers to him that which is good and lawful, also exposes its opposite, which is evil and forbidden; and the nature of good and evil, as it forms the foundation of human institutions, has been derived from our experience of their effects, or a calculation of their tendencies. The will of man, therefore, is as free as his experience dictates, and his reason urges to action: yet, that he should often act in opposition to both, is as lamentable as certain: in the transport of immediate gratification, or in the hopes of enjoyment, precept ceases to influence, and example loses its warning.

Video meliora proboque, deteriora sequor.

FOOTNOTES:

[12] In some of these instances, where the will has ceased to influence the muscles, the due sensibility of the nerves has remained.—Medico-Chirurgical Transactions, vol. ix. p. 8.

[13] So little does the infant appear to possess any control over those organs which afterwards become subject to voluntary influence, that it may be sufficient to remark the

flow of saliva, of urine, and the more solid evacuations, are subject to no restraint, and for some time are passed with little or no consciousness: even the motions which are excited in the limbs, appear to be spasmodic, rather than the effect of direction.

[14] Vide Darwin's Thesis de Spectris Ocularibus.

ON THOUGHT OR REFLECTION.

Those recollected objects, which have been transmitted by the senses, or which we have perceived by their means, are the subjects of our thoughts or reflections; for these terms will be indifferently employed, as designating the same faculty or process. The obvious meaning of the word *reflection*, is the representation of any object in a mirror. This term, so well understood in that department of natural philosophy named optics, has been transferred to mind, in order to explain a process, supposed to be similar. If, however, we examine the analogy, it will not accord:—to produce reflection in the mirror, the object must be present; in the mind, the reflection takes place when the object is absent. Although the simile, strictly speaking, is imperfect, yet the figure is beautiful, and, considering the metaphorical nature of language, as applied to mental operations, the most natural and appropriate that could have been selected; for, speaking in a general way, our thoughts, in themselves appear very much as the shadows or reflection of our perceptions. As we are but little capable of communicating the nature of our perceptions, independently of language, we must have recourse to inference and conjecture. It is fully understood that our visual perceptions, through the medium of recollection, may be represented by the skilful execution of the hand; and that those of smell, taste, and touch do not directly admit of such delineation. We might next inquire, if the odours we perceive are as strongly impressed on the olfactory organ, as the subjects of visual perception on the eye? Are they as fully and distinctly recollected? and are they capable by themselves of affording the materials for thought or reflection? Animals possess certain senses in common with ourselves; and, in many, the organs are more susceptible than our own; but there are no circumstances which have yet transpired, to induce us to suppose that the perceptions they have acquired are reviewed by their minds, when the objects which excited them are absent. The memory they possess of the perceptions they have experienced, is perhaps superior to that of human beings; still it does not appear, from any manifestations they afford, that it is actively exercised, as with ourselves, but occasionally excited by the recurrence of the object which originally produced it. Language is the pencil which marks the bold outline, and lends a colouring to our different perceptions; and with this boon man is exclusively gifted. A rational curiosity will prompt the reader to inquire, in what our perceptions consist independently of the language in which we ordinarily clothe them. In the instance of optical perception, we know that it is *something* which is retained by the memory, and may be traced by the hand, so as to convince others that it is truly remembered or recollected[15]; but let the same enquiry be made concerning the perceptions we receive by the touch, the smell, and the taste: in this investigation we shall experience much greater difficulty, as it is an endeavour to conceive the nakedness of a figure which is always clothed. That these perceptions must also be*something* abstracted from the terms which represent them, is proved, by the circumstance, that they are recollected when they occur again. As we are educated by language, and acquire a facility of employing it as the vehicle of our thoughts, we are little accustomed to contemplate the subject in this manner, and this also enhances the difficulty. When, however, the importance of speech is adequately considered, it will, I think, be detected, that the terms which we employ as the representatives of the perceptions of touch, smell, and taste, are the only media by which they can be voluntarily recollected or communicated to others; and, as signs of such perceptions, are equivalent to the representations by the hand of those which have been perceived by the organ of vision. To attempt the analysis of these silent deposits, to endeavour to describe these bare perceptions, would be altogether unavailing, because description implies language. In fact, it would be an effort to detect the symmetry of the human frame, by loading it with modern finery. The wonderful capacity which man exclusively enjoys, both for the communication of his thoughts, and for the improvement of his memory, in being enabled to acquire and transmit knowledge by impregnating sound with intelligence, and more especially in exhibiting its character embodied to the eye, leaves the rest of animated creation at a prodigious distance. This endowment of language to man, whereby he can, by an articulate sound, recall the perception of objects, (not indeed equal to the sensorial impression, but sufficient for their recollection, and also for the proof of their identity)—whereby he can with equal intelligence exhibit their character to the eye, is sufficient to explain of what the materials of his thoughts consist:—and to prove that animals being unable to substitute a term for their perceptions, are incapable of the process which we denominate thought or reflection. To fathom this mystery, is perhaps impossible; but, from attentively watching that which passeth within us,— from considering the state of animals which want this endowment altogether, it seems to be a law of our intellectual constitution, that our thoughts or reflections can only consist of the terms which represent our perceptions; and this is more evidently true, when we reflect on those subjects which are of a general or abstract nature.

Whoever will attentively watch the operation of his own mind,—for this subject admits of direct experiment,—will find that he employs terms when he conducts the process of reflection. In order to afford a fair trial, it is necessary that he should be alone, and subject to no interruptions. It will also add to the facility of the experiment, that he select a subject with which he is but little acquainted, as the process will be more deliberate. On topics with which we are familiar, we have acquired a rapidity of exercise which renders the detection of the process more difficult and perplexing. In this trial, he will be aware that he is repeating words as the materials of his thoughts. If the subject on which he should think involves persons with whom he is acquainted, or scenes he has viewed, he will, in addition to the terms he employs, have the pictures, or visible phantasmata, of these presented to his mind, conjunctively with such words. That we actually employ terms in this process is evident in many, who, when exercising their thoughts on any subject, are found, as we term it, talking to themselves; so that we are enabled to observe the motion of their lips: and this circumstance is to be noticed in most persons when they are counting.

The contrivances of language enable us to connect our thoughts; for our perceptions are distinct and individual, and of themselves can possess no elective attraction to*associate* and combine: they may however, by repetition or habit, become so allied, that the occurrence of one will excite the sequence of the other. We ordinarily recollect them very much in the order and succession of their occurrence; but we are also able to arrange and class them, and by such means, of recollecting them according to the artificial order of their distribution. This may be exemplified in the various expedients that have been devised for the acquirement and retention of knowledge: thus, chronology records events according to the order of their occurrence; an encyclopædia arranges according to alphabet or subject; and the most perfect of this kind, like the index to a book, consists in their mutual reference.

This wonderful faculty of thought or reflection, so far as we possess the means of detecting, appears to be peculiar to man; and if it be admitted to consist of our recollected perceptions, by the contrivances of language, we shall find that animals are not in possession of the necessary materials.

The ear transmits sounds to animals possessing this sense; and in some species it is so exquisitely susceptible, as to surpass, by many degrees, the acuteness of the same organ in the human subject. It is also recorded, that in some of the wilder tribes of man, the hearing possesses a delicacy of percipience unknown to the inhabitants of a polished community. Superadded to the conveyance of ordinary sound, the ear of man is the great inlet of communication, and the vehicle of articulate intelligence. Through the medium of this sense his knowledge becomes extended, and his memory improved; for every conversation is either a review of his stores, or an addition to his stock. As our thoughts or reflections are conducted by language, great caution is required that the terms we employ should possess a fixed and determinate meaning; and this is more especially important, when we employ words which are not the representatives of the objects of our perceptions, but of a complex nature, or, as they have been denominated, general terms; such as those which are used to designate the faculties and operations of the mind, and such as convey our moral attributes. The perfection of the process of thought, consists in the attention which the will can exert on the subjects of[16] consideration. The nature and endurance of the attention, which the organs of sense can bestow on the objects of perception, have been already discussed; and it will be found, that the same influence is directed when we exercise reflection: so that that mind is to be considered as most efficient, (in proportion to its natural capacity,) which can dwell on the subjects of its thoughts without interruption from irrelevant intrusions. The exertion of voluntary control over our thoughts has been denied; but if we were to subscribe to such doctrine, it would follow that this noble faculty of reflection would be merely a spontaneous concurrence of images and terms accidentally revived,—on rare occasions fortuitously blundering on wit, and ordinarily revelling in the absurdities of distraction. In proportion as we have been duly educated, we become enabled to direct and fix the organs of sense to the objects of perception, to be able at will to revive our memoranda, or to call on the memory to exhibit the deposits which have been confided to its custody, and to dwell pertinaciously on the materials of reflection. It is, however, certain, that in ordinary minds, the attention is little capable of being fixed to objects, and still less to the subjects of reflection; but this incapacity, in both instances, is principally to be attributed to the defects of education, and to a want of proper discipline of the intellectual powers. The endurance of attention in minds of the highest order, by a wise law of our constitution, is limited; and if it be attempted to continue the exertion beyond the natural power, the effort is infructuous. As straining the muscles produces fatigue, stiffness, and tremor;—as ocula spectra intrude on the forced and protracted attention of the visual organs,—so confusion ensues, when thought is racked and goaded to exhaustion.

As the staple of the human intellect is vastly superior to that of animals, so we find among our own species a considerable range of capacity; but however we may estimate mental excellence, it should be recollected, that its possession has seldom contributed to the happiness of the individual; so that experience would lead us to prefer the sober medium, which is included by a parenthesis, between the extremes of genius and dulness, and which appears to be the unenvied lot of the mass of society. The two great distinctions which mark the intellects of our species, seem to consist in the difference of character, which is established by those who excel in the exercise of their perceptions and consequent recollection, and those who cultivate and discipline the energies of thought. The former are distinguished by a vigorous activity, a penetrating and unwearied observation; their curiosity seems rather to be attracted by the object itself than directed by the mind. This incessant occupation and restless inquiry furnishes the memory with an abundant vocabulary: they recollect each object they have seen, and can retrace every path they have trodden; the ear greedily imbibes the conversations to which they are anxiously disposed to listen; that which they read, they verbally retain; they excel in quickness of perception and promptitude of memory, and appear to have every thing by heart; they are "the gay motes that people the sun-beams" of the intellectual world:—thus we find them, as inclination may sway, accurate chronologists, biographers pregnant with anecdote, expert nomenclators, botanists, topographers, practical linguists, and bibliographers; in short, the opulent possessors of whatever perception can detect, and memory preserve. The other order of men, (and they are comparatively few,) are the creatures of reflection:—with them the senses are little on the alert; they do not fatigue the wing by excursions through the field of nature; but that which the recollection retains becomes the subject of mental examination. An event is not registered from having merely occurred; but the causes which produced it are investigated, and a calculation is instituted concerning its probable tendency. Words are not simply regarded as the floating currency or medium of exchange, but they are severely subjected to analysis to establish their standard, or to detect the excess of their alloy; their senses are little awake to external impressions; the objects which a change of scene presents are slightly noticed, and feebly remembered; their curiosity is not attracted from without, but excited from within; they are strangers to the haunts of gay and mirthful intercourse, and are rather consulted as oracles, than selected as companions. This constant occupation of thought produces the philosophical historian, profound critic, physiologist, mathematician, general grammarian, etymologist, and metaphysician. After long exertion they become disposed to melancholic disquietude, and often turn in disgust from a world, the beauties of which they want an incentive to examine, and taste to admire. Both of these intellectual orders of our species contribute, but in different manners, to the stores of knowledge. The sound, efficient, and useful mind consists in a due balance and regular exercise of its different faculties.

How great soever the pains which an individual may bestow, to fix his thoughts to the examination of a particular subject, he will find that the effective duration of his attention is very limited, and that other thoughts, often wholly unconnected with the subject, will intrude and occupy his mind; on some occasions they are so prevailing and importunate, that he loses the original subject altogether. It is acknowledged, that the soundest and most efficient mind, is distinguished by the control it is capable of exerting on its immediate thoughts; which consist, as has before been observed, of terms, and the phantasmata of visible recollection:—this wandering of the thoughts to other subjects, or this intrusion of irrelevant words and pictures, whichever may be the case, appears to bear a very strong resemblance to a morbid state. It is usually the attendant on indolence, and has probably its source in a want of the proper occupation of mind, and, by indulgence, may become an incurable habit. Yet this rumination of mind has its votaries: by some it is courted as a delightful amusement, and eulogies are bestowed on the incoherent tissue of these reveries and day-dreams. Although these illegitimate offsprings of "retired leisure" may be considered as a perversion of the noblest attribute of man; yet they serve, in some degree, to recruit our recollection of past transactions, which might otherwise have faded in obscurity, or perished from natural decay. In the soundest and most refreshing sleep we seldom dream; so, in those wholesome exercises of the intellect where the mind is fully occupied, and, more especially, when such pursuit is combined with bodily exertion, these masterless associates do not intrude. By continuance, this habit may be so formidably increased, more especially under the guidance of malignant or depressing passions, that these shadows become embodied, and assume a form so potent and terrible, that the will is unable to bind them down, and the understanding attempts to exorcise them in vain.

The act of thought or reflection, therefore, appears to consist, not in the operation of an exclusive and particular faculty, but in the voluntary recollection of pictures, as far as visible perception is involved, and of terms or words which are the types or representatives of our perceptions, together with those general terms, which are to be considered as abbreviations of meaning or intelligence. All this would, however, only amount to an act of memory, of such pictures and terms, particular and general; and would not comprehend or include their analysis, estimate, admeasurement, or *ratio*, with inquiries into their source and tendency, which is denominated *reason*, and which will compose the materials of the following chapter. Suffice it to observe that our thoughts on any subject can only be according to the extent of our knowledge of things and opinions; and, therefore, that our thoughts or reflections necessarily involve our reasonings, as they are only recollections without them.

FOOTNOTES:

[15] In this capability animals will never rival us, as they are deficient of the *hand*, the operative instrument by which it is effected.

[16] It may be proper to explain the origin and meaning of this word, and of another usually employed in a similar sense, namely, contemplation. The former is compounded of *cum* and *sidus*, and presumes a fixity of mind adequate to the survey of the heavenly bodies; the latter is derived from *cum* and *templum*, and imports the same gravity and

concentration of thought which we carry to the fane of devotion.

ON REASON.

The opinions of the thinking part of mankind have been much divided concerning the signification of the term Reason. Every person, conceives himself privileged to reason upon all the subjects of human intelligence; and whatever he may chuse to offer on any side of a question, he denominates his reasons for or against it. By some, this power is held to be the exclusive possession of man; and such persons naturally conclude that an offence is offered to his intellectual dignity, if the smallest portion be conceded to the most docile animals. This is, however, a question for future examination, and will be discussed when their faculties are more particularly investigated. Those who have affirmed that our own species is exclusively gifted with reason, have not in any manner defined the nature of this faculty, or enumerated the steps of the process by which reasoning is performed: indeed, so ambiguous has been the signification annexed to this term, that it is not uncommon to meet, in the best authors, with the expressions of right reason, false or inconclusive reasonings, absurd reasons, &c. These epithets are, however, perfectly correct, as will be demonstrated in the course of this enquiry.

If this capacity of reasoning be peculiar to man, it would not appear difficult to trace the gradations of the process when he employs it: every act of intellectual exertion, deliberately performed, is attended with consciousness; he must therefore be aware of the successive steps of his march: but as this effort might be perplexing to minds unaccustomed to such deliberate and minute investigation, a readier method presents itself in order to attain the object. There are writers in all the departments of human knowledge, who are deservedly held in the highest estimation, and who have reasoned on the subjects they have treated, with the utmost correctness and ability:—let the best specimens of that, which, in these authors, is allowed to be reasoning, be selected and analysed, which will readily demonstrate the means they have pursued to arrive at their conclusion. The whole of this process being conducted by significant sounds conveyed to the ear, or in the signs of these sounds presented to the eye, the inquirer would be immediately impressed, that intelligent sound, or its character, that is, language, must be the vehicle by which this process is performed. In the next place, he would be sensible that these sounds, or their signs, were the substitutes or intended representatives of the objects in nature, either individually or collectively; for he would find that men, by the instrument of speech, had contrived, by a term, equally to express collections as well as individuals; as a man, or an army, which latter might consist of many thousands of the same beings. When he had arrived at this knowledge, he would be persuaded of the importance of these terms, and feel the necessity of their precise and uniform signification, as the representatives of the particular objects or collections they professed to describe:—because, if different significations were affixed to the same term, those who employed it could not mean the same thing. These prefatory observations appear to be proper, and it is important that the reader should bear them in mind; but it will be evident that the most correct description of objects does not constitute the process of reasoning, however indispensable it may be as its foundation.

Reason, as the term itself shows, implies *ratio*, estimate, proportion, or admeasurement; and in all the instances of reasoning that can be adduced, this interpretation will apply in the strictest sense. But *ratio*, estimate, &c. involve numbers, by which they can alone be characterised or defined. Thus, by way of illustration, the estimate for a building implies the number of the different materials, with their *cost*, which is the number of pounds, shillings, and pence; also the number of requisite workmen to be employed for such time, or number of weeks, days, &c. at a certain stipend: admeasurement also consists of numbers, whether it be employed on solids, fluids, or designate the succession of our perceptions, called time[17]: and ratio or proportion is equally the creature of numbers. In a preceding part of these contributions, the importance of numbers hasbeen considered, and a confident belief expressed that no animal is capable of numeration; and that the comprehension of addition and subtraction, the basis of all calculation is exclusively the province of the human intellect. This subject, however, requires a more extended investigation; and the research would doubtless reward the toil of the inquirer.

It is generally acknowledged, that arithmetic, or the combination and separation of numbers, is the purest and most certain system of reasoning, and liable, when properly conducted, to no difference of opinion; because the meaning of number is definite and universally agreed on, there being no nation that affixes a different value to the units, which are the elements of all ulterior numerative progression; and although, in different languages, they are called by different names, as Δεχα [Greek: Deka], *decem, dieci, dix,—taihun, tÿn, zehn, tien, ten,* yet they have an identical meaning, and denominate the same thing; and notwithstanding the Roman and Arabic symbols are of different character, they represent the same number, whether we employ X or 10. It is owing to this identity of meaning, that the reasoning in numbers is subject to no diversity of opinion.

The names of those things which have an actual existence, and can be submitted to the inquisition of our senses, or are capable of being analysed, are subject to comparatively little error, when we reason concerning them, because their character is defined by observation and experiment: but we have terms to designate that which cannot immediately be submitted to the analytic operations of our senses, and which has no palpable existence; and from the undefined nature of these, the greatest discord and confusion have prevailed when we reason concerning them; as the terms, humanity, charity, benevolence, living principle, organisation, materialism, political expediency, taste, liberty, legitimacy, and a thousand besides.

In order to proceed regularly with this subject, it appears that our reasonings may be employed concerning things, or the objects in nature, and on terms which are not the immediate representatives of natural phenomena, but as they have been denominated general or abstract; and which are intended to be the verbal representatives of multitudes of objects arbitrarily classed, or of opinions comprised under such term.

That reason is not an inherent, peculiar, and independent faculty of the human mind, receives a strong confirmation from considering, that it cannot be voluntarily exerted on subjects of discussion, but requires, as the indispensable condition of its operation, the basis of knowledge, which is to be understood to mean, the result of observation and experiment: for the mere employment of language, on a subject with which we are unacquainted, is but idle prating and a lavishment of words. To reason, is to adapt our means, that is, our knowledge, for the attainment of the end or object proposed: it is the estimate or admeasurement of these means. If, for example, a military commander intended effectually to bombard a city;—such being the object proposed, he would immediately proceed to estimate, admeasure, or calculate his means to produce the effect, and his success would depend on the knowledge he possessed of the nature and properties of the materials employed: he must calculate the distance, elevation, proportionate quantity of powder, and the time the fuzee should burn previously to the explosion of the shell; with various other necessary circumstances. This is an example of a very pure process of reasoning as applied to things, and accords with the definition that has been attempted. If it were necessary to multiply instances of the reasoning on things, perhaps the construction of a thermometer would be a well-adapted illustration; and it would likewise exhibit that which I am very anxious to impress, namely, the very gradual manner in which knowledge, by the operation of reasoning has been applied to the purposes of utility. That many substances, and particularly metallic bodies, augmented in magnitude by being heated, or, as we now term it, expanded by heat, was known many centuries ago, and was a fact of hourly occurrence to the artificers in metals. A similar increment of bulk was also observed in fluids; and it was likewise known, that their dimensions contracted as they cooled. This fact appeared to obtain so generally, that it became an aphorism, that bodies expanded by heat and contracted by cold. Of the precise gradations of heat they were, however, ignorant. Most of the senses became tests, although they were inaccurate criteria.

The sight conveyed some distinctive marks; so that when some metallic bodies were heated to a high degree, they were observed to become red, and as the heat was increased, they were rendered white. By the touch, a variety of discriminations of temperature was obtained, to which appropriate terms were annexed, explanatory of its effects, or according with the feelings; as burning, scorching, scalding, blistering hot;—descending to blood, loo, gently, or agreeably warm. The ear was not exempted from its share of information, by detecting the boiling of water, or by discovering when a heated metal was immersed in that fluid, that it was hissing-hot: even the smell detected some obscure traces, sufficient to discourage or invite an approach. These tests, although they might serve for ordinary purposes, were still wholly inadequate for philosophical accuracy. To ascertain quantity, it was necessary to associate number as the index of precision. Notwithstanding the construction of this instrument now appears so simple and easy of contrivance, it is only within a few years that it occurred to fill a tube, having a bulb, with a fluid; and to note the points at which snow dissolved, and water boiled: when these were fixed, the intermediate space might form a scale according to any subdivisions, so as to endow it with precision by the adjunct of numbers. On many occasions, our sensations deceive us, especially in a morbid state of the body: a person in the cold stage of an ague shivers at the temperature that oppresses his attendant with heat; but the instrument described is subject to no variations, by marking the gradations of warmth with the definite character of number. It will now be seen, that man possesses materials for conducting his reasonings, which animals do not enjoy;—by language, and from his capacity of numerating. Speech, of course, involves its record, whereby he can recall the transactions of former ages, and preserve the fruit of experience for his intellectual nurture, when the tree that produced it has perished. This record is the elaboration of the hand,—that wonderful instrument, the register of thought,— that active and and skilful agent that "turns to shape" the contrivances of the mind.

It is perhaps impossible, in a few words, to describe precisely the nature of the operation termed reasoning. In general terms it may be defined, *the means we employ for the attainment of the end proposed; the employment of knowledge for the discovery of truth*; or *the process of demonstration*; whether the object be an arithmetical sum, a geometrical problem, or a discourse on taste. A part of the process of reasoning, according to received opinion, consists in comparison, either of things, or of general terms; and this comparison implies not merely their exterior similitude, but likewise their internal structure and composition: because two mineral substances may resemble each other in external appearance, and may wholly differ in their intrinsic properties. The process of ascertaining wherein they agree, and the circumstances which discriminate them, is an instance of reasoning, or the means we employ for the proposed end, and which means necessarily imply the previous possession of knowledge. It will also be seen that in the instance adduced, and indeed in most others, where we reason on things, that precision can only be attained through the medium of number; for these mineral substances, although similar in external character, may contain very different proportions of the precious metals, and their actual value can only be estimated by comparison; that is, by an analysis, founded in knowledge, to ascertain the per centage of gold or silver, which must be expressed in numbers: and the comparison that is instituted concerning general or abstract terms, must have for its basis the establishment of their legitimate force and meaning.

When we consult authorities on this subject, and particularly Dr. Johnson's dictionary, we find that he has given eleven different significations of the term *reason*, which he defines to be "the power by which man *deduces* one proposition from another, or proceeds from premises to consequences." There is, however, much ambiguity in this statement; and it would perhaps be impossible, in reasoning concerning things, (which is to be considered as the most perfect example of this process,) to adduce an instance, in which one proposition is strictly *deduced* from another.

Every proposition is distinct, and independent: numbers, which are definite, may be added together, and the sum-total exhibited, or a lesser number subtracted from a greater, and the remainder shown. It is difficult to say what is really meant by the words "deduces one proposition from another." On examination, it will be found that every simple proposition contains some fact or dictum, something set up or laid down, *aliquid propositum*; and that nothing can be *deduced* from it, more than the meaning which the words constituting such proposition legitimately convey: indeed, it must be evident, that any deduction from a simple proposition would destroy its force. The sum of our knowledge consists of individual facts, which are in themselves distinct, as much as a flock of sheep is the aggregate of the different animals that compose it; and it is only a misapplication of language, to affirm that we are able to deduce one proposition from another. One proposition may tend to explain or illustrate another; but every proposition, correctly so termed, relates only to itself.

63

The other mode by which we reason, is on abstract or general terms, which are not the representatives of individual substances, or the objects of our perceptions; but the names of classes or collections, or of various hypotheses included or designated by a single name. The difficulties which environ this latter mode of reasoning become immediately evident, and satisfactorily account for the hostility and confusion it has engendered, and for the tardy advancement of real knowledge by this medium. The individual objects in nature can be investigated by observation and experiment, and may be sufficiently estimated; but multitudes of objects arbitrarily classed, or imaginary qualities comprehended by a single name, do not admit of the same analysis by the senses, and we are only enabled to ascertain their real meaning in the two ways that have been pointed out,—by authority, which, to be strictly such, ought to be invariable,—or by etymology, which will demonstrate their original signification, and the reasons which imposed them. Thus when we reason concerning charity, benevolence, humanity, and liberty, terms certainly of the highest importance, but each of which involves a variety of circumstances, and the real signification of which, is to this moment differently interpreted, we are impeded in the process, and fail in our estimate, because the dimensions are uncertain. That which one man considers a charitable donation, another views as the means which encourage idleness, and vice, and a third person is perhaps induced to question the motive, by attributing the gift to pride and ostentation. These general terms seldom admit the precision of numbers, but are characterised as to their proportions by expressions equally general and indefinite: as, much, more, and most, to denote their augmentation; and, little, less, least, to define their diminution. These general but indefinite degrees of comparison, as they are termed, once

64

defined the temperature of our atmosphere, until a scale was discovered to mark its increment and diminution by the accuracy of numbers. Great as may be the convenience of general terms, both for abbreviation and dispatch, they are notwithstanding liable to considerable suspicion, and are the frequent sources of error and misapprehension. It has been principally for this reason, that in proportion to the advancement of the physical sciences, the study of scholastic metaphysic has been deservedly neglected.

FOOTNOTE:

[17] Time, or the admeasurement of the successive order of our perceptions, embraces a wide area of definition; and it is perhaps impossible, in a few words, to circumscribe the range of its meaning. The sagacity of the human intellect, although by very slow gradations, has accumulated the wonderful mass of knowledge we now possess on this subject: and the investigations which have been made into the faculties of animals, justify the conclusion that its comprehension is limited to man. It would be highly interesting to trace the origin and progress of our information, concerning the nature of time; but a short note to a compressed essay, does not admit of such examination. However, it appears evident, that the striking and regular phenomena of nature have constituted some of our most important distinctions. Thus, the ebbing and flowing of the tide have formed a very early notation; and we still retain in our language the traces of its application in Whitsun*tide*, Shrove*tide*, Allhallow*tide*, &c. The great divisions of time are well understood; as day, from dawn; month, from moon; year, Anglo-Saxon gear, from gyrdan, the girth (of the zodiac). A moderate knowledge of the cognate languages of the north, would readily unravel the origin of all the terms that have been employed by us and

kindred nations, for the purpose of characterising the succession of our perceptions. All these subdivisions necessarily imply a comprehension of numbers.

From the experience of the past, man has inferred the *probability* of the future; for by natural knowledge, the probability, great as it is, can only be deduced. The certainty has descended from a higher authority. Although the grammar of our language has endeavoured to mark our predictions of the future by certain signs; yet these do not convey any definite intelligence of that which *is* to come. In this state of being, man may receive assurances of ulterior existence, but he cannot invest his predictions with the certainty of numbers. The signs of Will and Shall, the utmost boundaries of his future glance, are both verbs in the present tense, and only signify his immediate intention of performance, at a time which may *probably* arrive.

INSTINCT.

It has been endeavoured, in the foregoing pages, to describe the intellectual capacities of the human being, and to account for his superiority, from the peculiarity of his structure, and the extended faculties it has conferred. It has also been attempted to maintain, that man, thus gifted, is the architect of his own mind; with the hopeful expectation, that it may tend to the improvement of his culture, but more especially, to exhibit him as the creature of responsibility, in consequence of his ampler endowments: "for unto whomsoever much is given, of him shall be much required."

The mental phenomena which animals display is a subject of equal curiosity and interest; but it is to be lamented that they have not yet been sufficiently observed, or faithfully collected. Their anatomy has been minutely and diligently investigated, and the functions which have resulted from the peculiarity of their structure, in many instances, have been industriously developed; but an enumeration of their intellectual bounties, and faculties of improvement, are still wanting to complete their history. As we are able to trace the progress of mind, in the infant, from its feeble glimmerings to its bright effulgence in the maturity of man; so we can contemplate the inherent wisdom that directs the animal tribe:—a liberal portion, sufficient for their individual protection, and for the continuance of their race. This definite allotment of mental craft to animals has rendered them stationary, while man has no barriers opposed to his improvement; but, under the fostering auxiliaries of a free soil, wholesome instruction, and intellectual labour, continually advances. However vast his present treasure may appear, its accumulation may be safely predicted; and it is to be expected, or at least, it may be hoped, that his career in moral practice will be commensurate with his progress in science.

The human intellect, or the capacity of man for the accumulation of knowledge, has enabled him, in a great degree, to render himself the master of the animal creation; and more especially over those which dwell on the soil he inhabits or range in the atmosphere he respires: his authority or conciliation has little extended to the tenants of the deep. Many of the larger quadrupeds he has subdued, and thereby has become enabled to substitute the exertion of their muscles to relieve the toil and fatigue of his own: of the swifter, he has coerced the speed, for the anticipation of his wishes: the breed of many he has extensively multiplied, to prey on their flesh, or to become nourished by their secretions: his knowledge has been directed to the physical improvements of their race, and he has also relieved them from many infirmities and diseases, consequent on their domestication and labour.

The wonderful construction of animals is a fit subject for the serious contemplation of man: but the most striking and important lesson which it impresses, is the adaptation of their organs to the purposes of their destination, or the means they possess for the discharge of the offices they perform. This construction is throughout an exemplification of that which has been defined reason; and that it is perfect, may be concluded from its being the work of the Creator. It has been already observed, that the perceptive organs of many animals, especially the eye, the ear, and the smell, are more acute and vigorous, than those in the human subject: with us, the olfactory organ is considered as the lowest sense, but in some animals it appears to be the most important; and even in man, under certain privations[18], the smell has become a test of the nicest discriminations: indeed, so far as the senses are concerned as the importers of knowledge, animals appear to be gifted beyond our own species. Their memory is also more perfect, as might be expected, from the exquisite sensibility of their perceptive organs. The accuracy with which they recognise persons and places is in many instances really astonishing; and the certainty with which they retrace the most intricate paths, is a proof of the excellence of their local recollection, and of the attention they are capable of bestowing on the objects of their perceptions. This enduring attention is perhaps to be accounted for from their want of reflection, which so frequently diverts man from dwelling on the objects of his senses. Thus, a cat will undeviatingly watch the hole through which a mouse is known to pass, far beyond the time which man can exclusively devote to a subject of expectation. But here their superiority terminates. Their recollection is not refreshed, as in man, by the substitution of a name for the object of perception; much less have they any contrivance to record such intelligent sound, whereby man can preserve and transmit his perceptions. Thus whatever individual excellence animals may attain, they want the means of communicating, and of transmitting to their successors, and this sufficiently accounts for their stationary condition, and for the progression of man.

That animals are *incapable of the power* which has been termed thought or reflection is most probable. According to the interpretation that has been given of this faculty, they are deficient of the materials, or of terms, the representatives of perceptions; consequently of their abbreviations, and of the contrivances by which a proposition or sentence is constructed. That they understand some words, is evident; they know their own names, and, by certain sounds, can be made to stop or advance, to seize or let go, to rise up or lie down; but the extent of this intelligence is very limited, and altogether different from the comprehension of a sentence.

It is not improbable that they dream; and, at such times, the recollection of objects and scenes may be presented to them in visible phantasmata; and in the delirium of canine madness, they are observed to snap at imaginary existences; but this is far below the process that constitutes reflection, which consists in the capacity of reviewing the whole of our perceptions; and it has been endeavoured to point out that this can only be effected through the medium of intelligent sound, or its visible representative. If we were to contend for their capacity of reflection, we must, at the same time, acknowledge, that they do not appear to derive any improvement from the process; and to suppose them endowed with that which was nugatory, and contributed in no degree to their advancement, would be an idle and useless hypothesis. When not employed and directed by man, their lives are principally occupied in procuring food, and in the propagation of their species; and when their appetites are satisfied, theyrepose or sleep: when not guided by instinct, they seem to act from established habits, or the dictates of immediate impression. They are capable of considerable acquirements under the coercive tuition of man, and may be taught a variety of tricks for his amusement or profit; but they do not appear to comprehend their utility, or to hold these instructions in any estimation, as they never practise them when alone. The most accomplished bear would not dance for his own entertainment; and the learned pig never attempted to become a school-master to the hogs of his acquaintance.

It has been previously noticed, that in man, and most animals, there were movements of the highest importance to life, which were directed by the Author of the universe, and over which they had no immediate control, termed involuntary motions; so we find, in the tribe of animals, various mental endowments, especially tending to the preservation of the individual, and to the succession of the race, which are not the results of their experience. These have been comprehended under a general term, and denominated instinct. By instinct, is meant the display of contrivance and wisdom by animals, which tends to preserve them as individuals, and to maintain their succession; an intellectual exercise so perfect, that human philosophy has not pretended to improve; so unvaried, that the excellence of its performance cannot be exceeded, and is never diminished; a clearness of execution, that "leaves no rubs and botches in the work," but which, it may be presumed, is not even comprehended by the animal itself, as it does not possess the organs or capacity to acquire the rudiments of the science on which its operations proceed. As man, in his healthy state, is little conscious of his involuntary motions, so I should presume that animals possess but a feeble consciousness of their instinctive achievements. This may be a subject for subtle disputants to decide; but it appears certain, during the exercise of instinct, that their volition must be suspended. When sufficient observation has collected the intuitive wisdom displayed by animals, we shall then be able to *define* what is precisely meant by instinct; and, which is of much greater importance, to furnish their intellectual history, of which the definition is an abbreviation. One of the most useful contrivances of language, is its abbreviation for the purposes of dispatch; and a definition implies the fewest words into which its history can be compressed, for perfect discrimination and identity of character. Without disputing about a term, it may be noticed, that young ducks hatched by a hen, immediately on their developement, and often with a part of the shell still attached to them, make directly for the water; while the hen, who has performed the office of a mother, screams with alarm for the consequences. A she-cat, the first time she brings forth her young, proceeds to secure the umbilical cord of each kitten, with the caution of an experienced midwife. In both these instances, experience cannot be adduced to account for the performance. When the admirable texture of a spider's web is contemplated; will it be contended that this elaboration is the result of mathematical knowledge *acquired* by the spider? Have the dwellings of the beaver, and the construction of the honeycomb, their solution in the geometrical attainments of the fabricators? The examples which have been enumerated, (and they are only a few, among multitudes,) can only be accounted for, by maintaining, that these wonderful phenomena proceed from a degree of knowledge acquired by these animals, and are the result of such attainment; or that they are independently furnished with such propensities by the Creator. If it can be demonstrated that the animals displaying the greatest acts of intelligence, are unable to acquire the rudiments of the arts they practise, and cannot comprehend the wisdom they execute, there will remain but one conclusion—that they are the immediate endowments of God. Man has his instincts, although they are few, and these appear to fade as his reason advances; woman enjoys a more bountiful supply. The intellectual difference of the sexes is strongly pronounced: the female is more the creature of perception: man, of reflection:—the duties imposed on her, require less of thought and volition; and when she resembles man by their possession and exercise, she becomes less amiable and attractive. But this is abundantly compensated by the intenseness and constancy of her affections.

The gift of instinct to animals, does not exclude them from acquiring knowledge by experience; for their minds are capable of improvement, according to the extent of their capacities, and the intellectual organs with which they are furnished. The instinct which is allotted to them is mental possession which they could not have acquired, from the limited nature of their faculties. All their instincts are processes of the purest reasoning, but they do not originate from themselves; they are not, as in man, the elaboration of thought, the contrivance founded on the estimate of knowledge; but a boon,—an endowment, by which experience is anticipated, and wisdom matured without its progress and accumulation. Animals form an estimate of that which they can accomplish: a horse will not voluntarily attempt a leap he cannot clear; but his admeasurement is instituted solely by his eye: he is deficient of the organ which man possesses;—nor can he measure by steps or paces, as he is unable to numerate. An old hound will spare himself much fatigue in the chace, by knowing, from experience, the doubles of the hare. As man cannot reason independently of knowledge, nor beyond the extent of his acquirements, neither can animals display this faculty further than they possess the means.

The instinctive bounty of intellect to animals, of course, renders them stationary as a community; as instinct implies a definite portion of intuitive sagacity, wisdom, or reason, commensurate to their wants and destination. The early manifestation of instinctive wisdom, is the best reply to those philosophers who have argued against its existence; for in a multitude of instances it is exhibited, anterior to the possibility of experience. Man, although gifted with superior capacities, and susceptible of higher attainments, does not, from the paucity of his instincts, arrive during many years at the same maturity both of mind and body, which most animals display within the space of a few weeks; so necessary and important is the protracted period of infancy to the edifice and destination of the human mind.

FOOTNOTE:

[18] Notwithstanding we cannot sufficiently estimate the perfection of the senses in animals, yet in some instances we are enabled to observe, in our own species, the importance which a lower sense acquires, in consequence of the privation

of those which are deservedly considered the more noble. A singular case of this nature occurred in Scotland, the particulars of which have been published by Mr. James Wardrop an eminent surgeon and oculist, 4to. London, 1813. This person, James Mitchel, was born, very nearly blind and deaf. Although he was not deprived of every glimmering and vibration, yet he was incapable of discerning an object, or hearing an articulate sound; consequently to him the visible world was annihilated. A ray of light might serve to delight him as a toy, but it did not enable him to have the visible perception of any substance:—his nerves, indeed, appeared to be agitated by the concussion of sound, yet it was wholly impossible to lodge in his ear the missile of a word. Being thus deprived of the two nobler senses, his *mind* was constituted of the perceptions he acquired by the organs of touch, smell, and taste. His attention was enduring, and his curiosity eager, far beyond those of any animal. Mr. Wardrop observes that "his organs of touch, of smell, and of taste, had all acquired a preternatural degree of acuteness, and appeared to have supplied, in an astonishing manner, the deficiencies in the senses of seeing and hearing. By those of touch and smell, in particular, he was in the habit of examining every thing within his reach. Large objects, such as the furniture of the room, he felt over with his fingers, whilst those which were more minute, and which excited more of his interest, he applied to his teeth, or touched with the point of his tongue. In exercising the sense of touch, it was interesting to notice the delicate and precise manner by which he applied the extremities of his fingers, and with what ease and flexibility he would insinuate the point of his tongue into all the inequalities of the body under his examination.

"But there were many substances which he not only touched, but smelled during his examination.

"To the sense of smell he seemed chiefly indebted for his knowledge of different persons. He appeared to know his relations and intimate friends, by smelling them very slightly, and he at once detected strangers." From the whole of this interesting relation, it seems fair to conclude that this youth, even under the privation of sight and hearing, possessed, in the staple of his intellect, capacities beyond the most docile animals; and these consisted in the ardent curiosity which he displayed, and in his desire for the improvement of his limited faculties. Had this boy been confided to my management, I should have endeavoured to educate him through the medium of his touch, so as to communicate his wants, and afford an occupation to his mind. Thus, if milk had uniformly been served to him in a bowl, beer in a mug, water in a decanter with a glass stopper, and wine in a decanter with a cork: if these had been arranged in his apartment, he might have indicated his wish for any of these liquids, by producing the vessel that contained them: the two latter might have been subsequently abbreviated, by producing the glass stopper for water and the cork for wine. As he examined every object by the touch, it would have contributed both to his improvement and occupation, if he had been furnished with a quantity of ductile clay, which he might have modelled to represent the objects he examined, and which he might have preserved as a species of tangible vocabulary. According to my own suppositions, he might have been taught to numerate. It may be a subject of considerable curiosity to enquire, of what the reflections of James Mitchel could have consisted. He had no visible impressions which his hand could record. Being deaf, he could not have acquired the instrument of thought—language; therefore, for the objects of the senses he possessed,—smell, taste, and touch,—he could have no terms, as their substitutes, for the purpose of recollection. The next important question is, in what manner (wanting names whereby they might be represented) would the perceptions of smell, taste, and touch be represented to his mind in order to constitute reflection or thought on these experienced perceptions? If musk, rose, or garlic had been smelled, these perceptions, in a being constructed like Mitchel, would remain dormant, until the same odour were again presented to his olfactory organ; when it would be recollected, or he would be conscious, that it had been previously presented. In such a being, there would be a necessity for a fresh excitation of the organ of sense by the object, to produce recollection; whereas, in those who possess language, the name produces the recollection of the thing perceived.

CONCLUSION.

The subjects that have been discussed in these contributions, fully establish the pre-eminence of man, over all other created beings; and it has also been endeavoured to demonstrate the circumstances which have principally contributed to this superiority. The conclusions that may be drawn are equally important and consoling.

When the capacities of the intellect are fully ascertained, we shall be enabled to supply it with the proper materials of instruction; so that the protracted period of infancy may conduce to the formation of virtuous and enlightened members of civil society. The healing art will be abundantly promoted by a knowledge of mind;—for the remedy of its infirmities and perversions ought to be founded on a thorough knowledge of its faculties and operations;—nor should it be forgotten that the prevention of crimes, and the reformation of delinquents, equally involve an intimate acquaintance with the temperaments of human character.

In the contemplation of mind, from the highest order to the lowest rank,—from man, to the maggot that consumes him; we are imprest with the evidence of appropriate contrivance and infinite wisdom. Although we are unable to penetrate the dense veil, that conceals the arcana of vitality and intellect; yet sufficient is exhibited to us, in the ample volume of nature, to satisfy our curiosity, and stimulate the exercise of reason. Observation and experience have disclosed to us, in a great degree, the structure and functions of our own bodily frame; and the same persevering industry has unfolded the variations which obtain in animals. The conclusions that have been formed from the study of anatomy and physiology, amount to a conviction, that the contrivance is admirably adapted to produce the effects we behold;—that the means are competent to the end. The same reasoning applies to the phenomena of intellect, and may be illustrated by the comparative difference which appears in animals and man.

The mental endowments and capacities which animals possess, have rendered them stationary; whatever the more docile and intelligent may have been compelled to learn, they do not appear to comprehend, and want the means to communicate: so that their contemporaries and descendants are unbenefited by the acquirement, and the attainment perishes with the individual. When brought into existence, the world is to them a recent creation, and bears no evidence of a former race, from archives or monuments which they can understand. The record of their ancestors has been discovered by man, in fossile preservation; but its characters are unintelligible to them. As they have not been endowed with the capacity to numerate, they can experience no solicitude for the past, nor apprehension for the future. Their recollection is not an act of the will, but an excitation by the object that originally produced it. In the grammar of animals, the present is the only tense, and to punish them for the faults they had formerly committed, would be equally absurd and tyrannical. They are not the creatures of compact, and being unable to comprehend the nature of institutions, and the obligation of laws, they cannot be responsible agents. It has also been remarked, that they are destitute of sympathy for the sufferings of their fellows; but sympathy would be superfluous, where they cannot understand the nature of the affliction, and do not possess the power of administering relief.

The features of the human mind are very differently shaped, and strongly indicate an ulterior destination. Man possesses language, the instrument of thought, the vehicle of intelligible communication;—and he is gifted with the hand, to record the subjects of his experience, to fabricate his contrivances, and to rear the durable monuments of his piety and splendour. Thus, he is rapidly progressive, his mind becomes opulent from the intellectual treasures of his ancestors, and, in his turn, he bequeaths to posterity the legacy of wisdom. His comprehension of numbers, on which the nature of time is founded, enable him to revert to the transactions of distant ages, and to invest faded events with the freshness of immediate perception. He alone can embalm the past, and welcome the tidings of the future. Man alone is fitted to covenant, although he may occasionally waver in the performance. His exalted capacities, his comprehension of the law, constitute his responsibility: for where the conditions of the compact are not understood, there can be no disobedience or delinquency.

The helpless condition of the human infant, and the paucity of its instincts, apparently render it less favoured than animals;—but it was necessary, in order to constitute man a moral agent and a responsible being, that he should be the architect of his own mind. When born, he has every thing to learn; and a large portion of his existence is consumed to qualify him for his station in society. Had he, like animals, been gifted with intuitive wisdom, the donation would have been so perfect, as to render instruction superfluous;—and such endowment would have diminished the measure of his responsibility. The freedom of his will, by which is to be understood the impulse of reason, not the blind dictates of appetite, nor the sallies of tumultuous passions, renders him amenable. Such is the force of the human mind, that it can surmount the difficulties which situation and circumstances oppose to its improvement: so powerful is reason, that it can correct the prejudices of early tuition, and atone for crime, by the pursuit of honourable practice. Man alone can repent; he only can retrace the acts of former commission, and resolve on amelioration for the future. Thus we find that moral responsibility has its basis in the comprehension of Time. In proportion to our love and estimation of justice, we must be satisfied that, under the purest forms of human government, it is but imperfectly administered: the rewards and punishments in this life will ever be blended with the hopes and fears, the interests and passions, of our species; and there is much of evil, which human sagacity cannot detect. When we consider the attributes of the Deity and the nature of man, we can never be induced to conclude that the tribunals of this world are the courts of final retribution. Man bears in his intellectual construction the badge of moral responsibility, and, consequently, the germ of future existence: and the only incentive that can urge him to the advancement of science, and the practice of virtue, is the reward that Revelation has unfolded.

THE END.

www.ingramcontent.com/pod-product-compliance
Lightning Source LLC
Chambersburg PA
CBHW062054280526
45788CB00003B/1222